The Time for Miracles Is Now

# THE TIME

# FOR MIRACLES

# IS NOW

Jack Ensign Addington

DODD, MEAD & COMPANY

NEW YORK

ISBN: 0-396-06858-8
Library of Congress Catalog Card Number: 73-9271

Printed in the United States of America
by The Cornwall Press, Inc., Cornwall, N. Y.

# Preface

Why a book on miracles? Are miracles occurring today? And if they are, can we afford to ignore them simply because we do not understand them? Suppose we could understand them and make ourselves receptive to experience them in our own lives, would we not be foolish not to investigate these supposedly supernatural events?

Most of us have considered miracles, if we thought about them at all, as belonging to the remote past or, at best, some way-out bit of magic wrought by an equally way-out miracle worker. Even the religious brush them over lightly as the work of God and therefore to be taken on faith and not to be understood. Thus is stopped any further investigation into many dramatic changes and developments occurring in the lives of people today.

We live in an age when man is able to explore the face of the moon with reasonable safety and live for long periods under the sea because of an understanding of physical laws involved, laws covering every scope of human activity. Today, nothing physical or mental is considered too mysterious to understand, yet, when an instantaneous healing of a physical condition occurs, it is brushed over as being an emotional phenomenon or something which defies explanation. Must a miracle be beyond explanation?

I live with miracles every day. I have seen so many that they no longer surprise me. This is not to say that I am not continually thrilled to watch the miracle-working Power at work in the universe. The past twenty-five years in the field of Spiritual Mind Healing have convinced me that man can experience whatever he can believe if he is willing to turn to the Power that is able to do all things for him. Jesus said that all things are possible to him who believes. Believes what? There are spiritual laws at work in the universe that perform with the same unfailing accuracy as the mental and physical laws we have come to take for granted. The only difference is they operate on a higher plane, a plane that transcends the mental and physical laws. When we involve the spiritual law through spiritual mind healing, and the spiritual law transcends the physical law, we say that a miracle has taken place. To understand something about the spiritual law is to understand *why* miracles take place. Did you ever stop to think that what seems like a miracle to us might be a thoroughly understandable and law-abiding event in the Mind of God?

Years ago when I studied law, a wise professor whose name was Forrest Cool used to start each course with: "Let's define our terms." Then we would take one term after another and spend weeks developing a foundation for understanding them. We took such a long time defining our terms that, before they were through, some of the students felt as if they must have had the entire course. When, at last, not only the terms but the principles upon which they were based were understood, it was easy to go through the legal cases. Now we had a foundation of understanding.

And so I say to you, as we begin this book on *The Time for Miracles Is Now,* "Let's define our terms!"

What is a miracle? A miracle is any dramatic change in body or affairs that appears to be supernatural because it is beyond explanation. I like Dr. Leslie Weatherhead's definition:

A miracle is a law-abiding event by which God accomplishes His redemptive purposes through the release of energies which belong to the plane of being higher than that with which we are normally familiar.

Redemptive means being redeemed from our foolish ways and brought back to the wholeness and perfection that is rightfully ours. It is what Jesus meant by *Be ye therefore perfect, even as your Father which is in heaven is perfect;* [1] it is: *Thy faith hath made thee whole;* [2] it is when the Truth has made us free; it is the transcending of physical law through the higher or Divine Law.

Throughout this book you will find the word "perfect," and people will say: "How can life be perfect when it is filled with sin, sickness and all manner of suffering?" Human judgment considers the word "perfect" a relative term. I am using it as Ultimate Perfection which is at the center of all Life. Plato called it the "Divine prototype." I repeat the words of Jesus: *Be ye therefore perfect even as your Father which is in heaven is perfect.* It was an understanding of the Divine Perfection which enabled Jesus to

1 Matthew 5:48.         2 Matthew 9:22.

perform instantaneous healings. Even a glimpse of Perfection is reflected as some manner of healing in the lives and affairs of men and women.

What is a spiritual mind treatment? Spiritual mind treatment is scientific prayer. It is an individual thought process whereby man's thinking is directed away from the need or problem and put in direct alignment with the Divine Mind, thereby enabling him to express his highest good. Spiritual mind treatment, whether for the self or another, is a clarification of the mind so that the divine perfect action of Universal Mind Power can come through. It is what Emerson meant by getting the bloated nothingness out of the way of the Divine circuit.

What is spiritual mind healing? Spiritual mind healing is a healing accomplished through a changing of the mind. It is an establishing of a consciousness of wholeness in the invisible realm of Mind that is bound to produce a corresponding effect upon the body or affairs. Man is a triune being. He is Spirit, living in a mental world, expressing on a material level through body.

What is Universal Mind Power? Universal Mind Power is an all-inclusive term encompassing all that God is: omnipresent, omniscient, and omnipotent. Omnipresent means everywhere present. There is no place where God is not. Omniscient means all-knowing, encompassing all Wisdom and Intelligence. Omnipotent means all power. *All power is given unto me in heaven and in earth,*[3] said the man who best understood the omnipotence of God. He meant that the infinite Power was his to use in heaven which he defined clearly as *within you* and in earth, the outer ex-

3 Matthew 28:18.

pression. Every treatment should be based upon an awareness of the three omni's, as well as the attributes of God. Man, created in the image of his Maker, inherits these attributes: Spirit, Mind, Life, Truth, Peace, Light, Power, Joy, Wholeness, Beauty.

What is a demonstration? A demonstration is any change in the physical, material or visible circumstances that is the manifestation of an awareness of one's inner perfection. It is the evidence of Truth realized in consciousness. Any healing of mind, body, or affairs is commonly called a demonstration.

This book is for the purpose of helping people to understand their true nature and live it. For too long man has allowed himself to be a pawn of the elements of the world and has not taken his rightful position as a true son of God. The Bible tells us that man is made in the image and likeness of his Maker, endowed with all of His attributes. *So God created man in his own image, in the image of God created he him; male and female created he them. And God blessed them and said unto them, Be fruitful and multiply and replenish the earth and subdue it; and have dominion over the fish of the sea, and over the fowl of the air, and over every living thing that moveth upon the earth . . . . And God saw every thing that he had made, and, behold, it was very good.*[4]

In its deep esoteric meaning, this means that we are to have dominion over our conscious thoughts (the birds of the air), as well as over our subconscious thoughts (the fish of the sea), and the effects of life (every living thing that moveth upon the earth).

[4] Genesis 1:27, 28, 31.

*By their fruits ye shall know them.*[5] In this book I intend to show that man need not remain in bondage to his own negative thinking, nor to the conditions and circumstances he has ignorantly brought upon himself.

"Man is not the creature of circumstances; circumstances are the creatures of men," said Benjamin Disraeli. And Paul said to the Galatians, *Stand fast therefore in the liberty wherewith Christ hath made us free, and be not entangled again with the yoke of bondage.*[6] We are talking about spiritual freedom, the freedom of the sons of God. All of us need to stop now and then and remind ourselves that we are not in bondage to circumstances, nor to situations involving people. No, not even to conditions of the body that sometimes seem so real.

We are free with the freedom of the sons of God, children of the Most High. As such, we have been given dominion over our lives and our circumstances. Right within our self-imposed bondage, we can find the freedom that we seek. Once we find our freedom within, the outer must always conform to the inner. If it takes a miracle, well and good. The time for miracles is now!

Jack Ensign Addington

[5] Matthew 7:20.                    [6] Galatians 5:1.

# Contents

# The Time for Miracles Is Now

# ONE

## I Discover Spiritual Mind Healing

*I know thy works: behold, I have set before thee an open door, and no man can shut it: for thou hast a little strength, and hast kept my word, and hast not denied my name. After this I looked, and, behold, a door was opened in heaven.*
—Revelation 3:8; 4:1

My interest in Spiritual Mind Healing began in 1945. At that time I was a practicing attorney employed as a counsel for a large insurance company in Los Angeles. My first wife, Patricia, who had always been quite frail, had developed a disease which the doctors diagnosed as a complete degeneration of the nervous system. The condition was considered by the medical profession to be terminal and she had been given about one year to live, a very unpleasant one at that for she could hardly be said to be enjoying life at all. She was extremely nervous, could not associate with people at all, not even to going to the market or having her friends come to see her. She shook as one who has Parkinson's disease. She was fearful, bordering on an anxiety neurosis, bedridden most of the time, listless, had no color in her face. You might say, she had given up living already. Once a week she visited a medical clinic and was

1

given drugs for the purpose of reducing the pain and alleviating the symptoms. All this was very distressing to me, our son, and the other members of the family. We all longed to help her but it seemed that nothing could be done.

## We Embark on a Great Adventure

And then, a wonderful thing happened. She began to listen to Dr. Dan Custer's daily radio program. Dr. Custer was an advocate of Spiritual Mind Healing. In fact, he claimed that there were no incurable diseases; that there was no condition that could not be healed through Spiritual Mind Healing. Pat became more and more interested in what this man had to say and wrote for Dr. Custer's home-study course. I began to notice a change in her. Color had come back into her cheeks and she was taking more interest in life in general. Then, one day when I came home from the office, she announced to me that she was going to depend upon Spiritual Mind Healing entirely. I was pleased to hear that she had laid out a program of exercises for herself, that she was going to start out by walking around the block each day. This was a tremendous right about face. "Something happened to me this morning when I was listening to Dr. Custer," she said. "All of a sudden I just knew I was going to get well." And she did. Each day she walked a little bit farther until she was walking over a mile a day. Already she was a different person.

Dr. Custer was lecturing every Sunday morning in Los Angeles and so we attended these lectures. We also began to read everything that we could get our hands on on the subject of Spiritual Mind Healing. Imagine our surprise to find that many people had been healed from all manner of so-called incurable diseases. And so our faith grew and it became more and more evident that Pat was not only getting better but was being healed through the study of this new (to us) philosophy. Finally, when there was no trace of her former condition remaining, we realized that she had, indeed, been healed. Her friends were amazed, more so than we who had witnessed the gradual change. She had become a completely changed person with a real zest for living. No evidence remained of her former condition.

*One Year Later*

It is interesting to note that one year from the time that she had first been given the ultimatum that she had only a year to live, she went back to the same medical clinic and presented herself for examination. When they pulled her file and compared the reports of her present examination with those of the year before, the doctors could not believe that she was the same person. They wanted to know what she had done. The doctor in charge of her case was a very religious man, and when he was told that this healing had come about through prayer, he nodded his head slowly in agreement. "Only the Lord could have healed this woman," he said.

I would like to go on record as saying that the healing of Pat's condition was a permanent healing. Some years later she made her transition from this life to the next under entirely different circumstances.

## A Whole New Way of Thinking for Me

During the year that we watched Pat's dramatic healing take place, a year spent in spiritual study and contemplation, a great change took place in me. I, too, became an entirely different person. It came as a revelation to me that this philosophy of Spiritual Mind Healing was more than just a means of bringing about a physical healing—it was a whole new way of thinking and living, a way of life that had become so all-absorbing to me that I could think of little else.

I took a year's leave of absence from my law practice and devoted all my time to study and spiritual growth. I never went back to the business world. Thus ended my first career—twenty years in the business world. My life seems to be divided into twenty-year periods. I then went into the ministry and taught and lectured on Spiritual Mind Healing for the next twenty years. I retired from active church work in 1968 and am now into my third twenty years—or more—with a worldwide healing ministry. During the twenty-six years I have been actively engaged in the work of Spiritual Mind Healing, I have seen so many dramatic changes take place in peoples' lives that nothing surprises me. Yet, there is always a feeling of wonder at the way the Power works, transforming the lives of men and women when they turn to It.

*Healing the Whole Man*

Spiritual Mind Healing is the healing of the whole man. To be more accurate we might say, the recognition in mind of that man who is already whole and perfect. Spiritual Mind Healing may be instantaneous. Many such healings are considered to be miracles simply because medical science is unable to explain them from the scientific viewpoint. Some Spiritual Mind Healings, such as Pat's healing, emerge gradually over a period of time. A true spiritual healing takes place through the changing of the mind. *Repent, the kingdom of heaven is at hand.*[1] To repent is to change one's mind and take a right about face in one's attitude to life. This is what happens when one is ready to accept a Spiritual Mind Healing. The Kingdom of Divine Right Action is always *at hand*. When spirit and mind are in harmony, the healing takes place through the visible third in the trinity which is body. Every Spiritual Mind Healing, regardless of how miraculous it may appear, is based upon scientific laws. Every healing must take place in mind before it can appear as an effect in the body. We can therefore say: Every healing whether it is effected through the ministrations of a medical doctor, the mental practitioner, or a miracle at Lourdes, has this in common— *It was first accepted in mind by the person healed.* This I have learned after working with thousands of people. Many are healed, some are not. It is still a matter of *Thy faith hath made thee whole.*[2] This is what led me to write this book. In it I hope to give enough evidence for Spiri-

1 Matthew 3:2.                    2 Mark 5:34.

tual Mind Healing so that anyone reading it can believe enough to accept a healing for himself.

## Nothing Too Difficult for Universal Mind Power

There is no disease, no problem known to man, whether it is of human relations, bondage to unhappy or limited circumstances of any nature, that cannot be healed through Spiritual Mind Healing. You can be healed from any physical condition; from a belief in poverty; from a lack of harmony in the home; from confusion and hostility in your office. Nothing is too difficult for God.

If you really want to be healed, you can find your healing before you finish reading this book.

"Of course I want to be healed!" you answer. But, do you? Are you sure there are no hidden secondary gains to your illness that you are protecting? Often, hidden from ourselves, these secondary gains pass unnoticed, yet they keep us from accepting the healing that we say we desire. Suppose we take a searching look at a few of them.

1. The need to punish the self. Among these are the personalities who seek to assuage their guilts through self-punishment, religious fanatics, such as flagellants, those who literally and figuratively wear the hair shirt and beat themselves to the point of drawing blood in order to do penance. Today, various kinds of sickness serve the same purpose for these masochistic personalities who draw to themselves injuries, illness, and suffering, in order that they may punish themselves.

2. The medical whip used as a power wedge over some member of the family. Here we have the mother who has a heart attack in order to keep daughter from leaving the nest. Even more common is the mother who refuses to share her son with a younger woman— the threatened heart attack is enough to keep him from marrying.

3. The responsibility dodger is seen in many guises. Sometimes it only takes a broken arm to save him from facing up to some responsibility at the office. Having a cold can be a convenience at inventory time.

4. The need to be a martyr. The parent who has worked his fingers to the bone for the family and now feels he or she deserves to be taken care of by the children, "It's my turn now." There is great enjoyment in casting one's self in the tragic role, enjoying the sympathy of friends and relatives.

5. Sickness draws concern from the family and substitutes for lack of love. Unconsciously a neglected member of the family may seek to gain the love he craves in this way.

6. The attention getter is a frustrated prima donna. He finds his ailments an ever ready subject for interesting (?) conversation and can always be counted on for a good "organ recital." He secretly rejects a healing because he'd hate to give up the drama of reciting those interesting symptoms.

7. A claim to fame. "No one has been able to help me yet!" he boasts. "The doctors are completely baffled by my case," he tells you. "They've never seen any-

thing like it!" He offers you the challenge of having a try at helping him, but secretly he doesn't want to give up his claim to fame.

8. Getting even, proving a point, and punishing somebody else. "I wouldn't be sick if we'd stayed in California where we belong," the wife says. Or, "I told you I was allergic to house dust and shouldn't do my own housework." And how about the husband who strains his back when asked to work in the yard? Eighteen holes of golf wouldn't hurt him a bit.

9. The accident prone. And how do you help the accident-prone victim who actually prides himself on his many accidents without realizing that he draws them to himself. Psychologists have proven that certain personalities do attract accidents for various reasons relating to the secondary gains we have been discussing.

*The Secret of Spiritual Mind Healing Is Available*

The Secret of Spiritual Mind Healing lies within these pages. It is a secret that has always been known by a few down through the ages, but it is a secret now available to every man and woman who is willing to accept it. This secret is not complicated. Actually, its very simplicity has caused it to be surrounded by superstition. It is the simple approach that is most successful. Start by knowing that there is something you can do. You, too, like Pat, can refuse to accept the prognosis. You do not have to stand and wring your hands and weep. You can decide to accept a Spiritual Mind Healing for yourself. It is a matter of letting the Power work through you through the changing of your mind. This book will show you how.

If you can accept a healing for yourself, a healing in any area of mind, body, and affairs, read on. It may come so suddenly that your doctor, psychologist, or counselor will be amazed. It may come so gradually that you will forget you ever had the problem and only years later realize that a healing has taken place. If you can accept it in mind and remove your own mental blocks that have been keeping you from experiencing the healing, you could possibly be healed before you finish this book.

# TWO

## The Many Avenues of Spiritual Healing

*Be thou made whole.*—Jesus

Believe it or not, you can be the instrument through which some person can receive a miraculous healing. You need not be a religious fanatic; you need not belong to any certain religious sect in order to be a *healer*. The healing may seem to come through your efforts, but this is a paradox, for a prerequisite of the art of healing is the certain knowing that *Of myself I do nothing, the Father within doeth the work*. Still, you can be the *door* through which another accepts the necessary faith. There is a Power greater than you are, a Power that resides in every part of life, a Power to which nothing is impossible, that will act through you and for you, according to your belief. Perhaps a look at the healing art down through the ages will enable us to understand better the universality of Spiritual Mind Healing.

*A Look at Some of the Ancient Healers*

One of the most fascinating of the great healing centers of antiquity was in ancient Greece. It was founded upon the Greek healing cult of Aesculapius. Aesculapius was supposed to be the son of Apollo, god of healing. Homer calls him the "blameless physician." Many temples were built to Aesculapius throughout Greece. The most famous of these temples was at Epidaurus. In the center of the compound was a beautiful shrine housing a gold and ivory statue of Aesculapius. The divine physician was represented as a seated figure holding in one hand the serpent-wound staff that is used as a medical insignia today. Grouped around this shrine were large airy buildings for the lodging of pilgrims and the care of the sick. The method of healing used here was most unusual, far different from anything that we know today.

The sick, having been received for healing, were put through a special routine in preparation. Clothed in new white garments, they were brought from their rooms into the big temple room built around the statue of Aesculapius. There they were left on their couches for the night. Their diagnosis was given to them through dream experiences; as they slept they saw the god come to life and walk among them prescribing the necessary remedies. In the morning the patients would tell their dreams to the physicians who would prepare the medicines. A disgusting example of primitive superstition, you say? Perhaps so. The interesting thing was that the sick recovered. Usually, at the end of the third day, they walked out healed.

*Testimonials Were Recorded Even Then to Increase the Confidence of Patients*

In ancient Greek inscriptions upon tablets in the temples, we find accounts of outstanding healings recorded for posterity.

Among these healings we find that when a boy, who was dumb, made his offering at the altar, he was asked by a torchbearer of the god if he would promise to make the usual thank offering if he was healed. The boy said, "I promise." To the amazement of all the bystanders, he had recovered his speech at that very instant.

The healing of a blind man is recorded. The man was blind in one eye. His eyeball was entirely gone, leaving only the lid. As he slept he was visited in his dream by the god, who seemed to boil a drug and put a poultice on his eyes. The next day he saw with both eyes.

The tablets also had the record of another blind man named Alcetas of Alicos. He dreamed that the god visited him and opened his eyes with his fingers so that he saw for the first time the trees about the temple. The next day he could see.

It is recorded that Hermon of Thasa, too, was cured of his blindness. But he failed to make the thank offering which he had promised. His blindness returned; but when he again promised to make the offering, he found that his sight was given him again.

## You've Heard of the Hippocratic Oath?

Perhaps you have seen in some doctor's office a framed copy of the famous Hippocratic Oath. It is a code of medical ethics, still taken by some recipients of the medical degree. Hippocrates, known today as the Father of Medicine, was born on the Greek island of Kos in the year 460 B.C. He was the seventh in lineal descent from the "divine physician," Aesculapius. His father was a priest physician and so was Hippocrates. When he had completed his education he took his vows before the altar of Aesculapius. He was considered then to be a member of the Aesculapiadea or Aesculapian cult.

Although Hippocrates is credited with writing over eighty-five books on the healing art, some people today doubt whether he actually existed. Like with Shakespeare's, there seems to be some mystery surrounding his vast work. Yet the cult of Aesculapius continued for centuries, the Romans, too, building a sanctuary to Aesculapius and reporting on tablets many healings.

The great Mystery Schools of antiquity, the sources of most that we know and believe, taught that the human consciousness was limited only by the arbitrary intellectual boundaries which it imposed upon itself. Is this impossible? Has the modern materialistic thinker really tried to explore the depths of himself? Has he sincerely examined all evidence which is *against* his own opinion? Has he *disproved* miracles, magic, clairvoyance, spiritualism, and telepathy? . . .

As time goes on medicine will depend less and less on harsh drugs to accomplish its results. Already the motion is well under way. Gradually the mind and its power will take the place of many revered remedies. Then we shall find out that there is something even deeper than the mind, and so we shall go on in our cautious crablike motion toward the world of spirit.[1]

## Healings Often Attributed to Sacred Relics

Numerous healings have been recorded based on the possession of some religious relic. There have been miraculous cures because people believed that they had in their possession a sliver of wood that was supposed to have been part of the cross. Dr. Thomson Jay Hudson in his book *The Law of Psychic Phenomena* brings out that the interesting thing is that it made no difference whether or not the relic was authentic. *If the patient believed that he had in his possession the sacred relic and had faith in it, he experienced a healing.*

Paracelsus stated what is now an obvious scientific fact when he uttered these words:

"Whether the object of your faith be real or false, you will nevertheless obtain the same effects. Thus, if I believe in Saint Peter's statue as I should have believed in Saint Peter himself, I shall obtain the same effects that I should have obtained from Saint Peter. But that is superstition. Faith, however, produces miracles; and whether it is a true or a false faith, it will always produce the same wonders."

Much to the same effect are the words uttered in the sixteenth century by Pomponazzi:

"We can easily conceive the marvellous effects which confidence and imagination can produce, particularly when both qualities are reciprocated between the subjects and the person who influences them. The cures attributed to the influence of

[1] Manly Palmer Hall, *Healing: The Divine Art* (New York: The Citadel Press, 1944).

certain relics are the effect of this imagination and confidence." [2]

Of the same nature are healings reported today from the possession of "prayer cloths" that have been blessed by some healers. This practice had its origin in Acts 19:11, 12: *And God wrought special miracles by the hands of Paul: So that from his body were brought unto the sick handkerchiefs or aprons, and the diseases departed from them, and the evil spirits went out of them.*

### Even Kings Were Said to Be Healers

Kings of England and France were supposed to be kings by divine right and therefore to have the power of healing. Up until the time of the French Revolution, the sick would present themselves to the king for the healing touch and many healings were said to have taken place. No matter how materialistic, how dissolute, the king, some who believed that they would be healed found that he did, indeed, have the *healing touch.*

Pyrrhus, king of Epirus, had the power of assuaging colic and affections of the spleen by laying the patients on their backs and passing his great toe over them. The emperor, Vespasian, cured nervous affections, lameness, and blindness, solely by the laying on of his hands. According to Coelius Spartianus, Hadrian cured those afflicted with dropsy by touching them with the points of his fingers, and recovered, himself, from a violent fever by similar treatment. King Olaf healed Egill on the spot by merely laying his hands upon him and singing proverbs. The kings of England and France cured diseases of the throat by touch. It is said the pious Edward

[2] Thomson Jay Hudson, *The Law of Psychic Phenomena,* 30th ed. (Chicago: A. C. McClurg & Co., 1905).

the Confessor, and, in France, that Philip the First were the first who possessed this power. In England the disease was therefore called "king's evil." In France this power was retained till within a recent period.[3]

## It Didn't Begin and End With Jesus

Many people think that healing was the exclusive domain of Jesus. It is true that Jesus was the instrument for many miraculous healings, healings of every sort, but he, himself, denied that he was the healer. *Of myself I do nothing,* he said, *the Father within me doeth the works.* He instructed the disciples in the art of spiritual healing and it is recorded:

And when he had called unto him his twelve disciples, he gave them power against unclean spirits, to cast them out, and to heal all manner of sickness and all manner of disease.

And he called unto him the twelve, and began to send them forth by two and two; and gave them power over unclean spirits;

And they cast out many devils, and anointed with oil many that were sick, and healed them.

And these signs shall follow them that believe; In my name shall they cast out devils; they shall speak with new tongues; They shall take up serpents; and if they drink any deadly thing, it shall not hurt them; they shall lay hands on the sick, and they shall recover. . . .

And they went forth, and preached every where, the Lord working with them, and confirming the word with signs following. Matthew 10:1; Mark 6:7, 13; 16:17, 18, 20

In his short ministry—barely three years—Jesus was instrumental in healing so many that it would take a book in itself to discuss just those healings recorded in the Gos-

[3] Ibid.

pels. There were many, many more that we will never hear about.

And there are also many other things which Jesus did, the which, if they should be written every one, I suppose that even the world itself could not contain the books that should be written. John 21:25

But it did not stop there, for then He trained seventy in the art of healing. Actually, the Bible says: *The Lord appointed other seventy also.*[4] So there may well have been various groups of seventy—seventy, that mystical number of Divine Perfection.[5] And the seventy were successful in their healing mission, returning filled with joy to report that even the devils were subject unto them through the Christ.

But, even before Jesus, healing was an accepted fact in Bible times. What about the healings attributed to Elisha, Elijah, and to Isaiah?

### The Healings at Lourdes Are Well Documented

One time when Adela Rogers St. Johns, the famous writer and author of many best sellers, was visiting us, she told me this story. She said:

I went to a monastery near Yonkers one time to do some research and while I was there came to know one of the Fathers in charge well. So one day I had an opportunity to ask him something that had bothered me for a long time.

"Father," I said, "why did the Blessed Virgin choose to appear in the Grotto of Lourdes to a girl named Bernadette?

---

[4] Luke 10:1.
[5] Jack Ensign Addington, *The Hidden Mystery of the Bible* (New York: Dodd, Mead & Co., 1969).

Bernadette was a peasant, she was ignorant, she was the lowest student in her class at school. She lived in a hovel where the people spoke with a dialect, she had asthma badly, she was as a rule none too clean. Why of all the world did Our Lady choose to appear to Bernadette?"

"Oh," the Father said quickly, "the Blessed Lady didn't appear to Bernadette."

This startled me and I said, "But, Father, the whole story of Lourdes is founded on the fact that the Blessed Virgin appeared there to Bernadette."

"No, no," he said, "you have it all wrong. The Blessed Virgin didn't appear to Bernadette. Bernadette could see her!"

Adela's face shone as she repeated the priest's words again to me.

"Don't you see?, don't you see?" she asked me. And then she added: "It took me a moment to appreciate the great difference. When I did I found in it a true blessing."

And so it all began. It was in the south of France that this took place back in 1858. Bernadette, at first, was considered to be a sort of freak for having such a peculiar experience. The other children went with her and again she alone saw the vision. Others began to take note of it and when she went to the Grotto to pray as many as ten thousand people went there, too, to watch her. At first, the authorities were very skeptical that this little peasant girl with no education could have had such a vision, but when she told them that the Virgin Mary referred to "the Immaculate Conception" they marveled that she should know such words of herself. The vision told Bernadette to bathe in the spring and "to go tell the priests to build a chapel here." After this, the Vatican, satisfied that Bernadette had been visited by the Virgin Mary, built a huge basilica at

Lourdes, with elaborate machinery to boost the flow from the spring and with seperate immersion pools for men and women.

The Catholic Church has been very cautious about verifying the healings at Lourdes so that out of some five thousand reported healings only about sixty-two have been authenticated. From what I have read of the process they go through to document one of these healings, it would seem that it is almost as hard to have a healing authenticated as to have a person canonized as a saint. However, those who are healed, authenticated or not, know that they have been healed and many others surrounding them know of the healings also. From the very first there were healings, dramatic healings.

I think that the healing of Madame Marie Biré as told by Ruth Cranston in her book, *The Miracle of Lourdes*,[6] is one of the most spectacular of all of the healings that have been reported and accepted by the church. Madame Biré, from Lucon, hardworking mother of six children, suffered fiendish headaches, dizziness, and was finally stricken with blindness. When she went to Lourdes, the physicians' reports showed that the optic nerve was completely atrophied. At the Grotto which she visited in an invalid carriage she suddenly stood up and said, "Ah, I see the blessed virgin!" She fell back into the carriage seat, fainting. Her daughter thought that she was dying. But her mother quickly recovered consciousness and found that she could see. The next day ten doctors examined her and reported that the organ was atrophied and lifeless, yet the sight clear and perfect.

[6] Ruth Cranston, *The Miracle of Lourdes* (New York: McGraw-Hill, 1955).

"How can you see, madame, when you have no papillae?" one doctor asked impatiently.

"Listen, doctor, I am not familiar with your learned words," she replied with spirit. "I have just one thing to say. For nearly six months I could not see, and now I can see. That is enough for me!"

This reminds us of the man who was blind from birth, healed by Jesus. When the Pharisees questioned him, he answered: "One thing I know, that whereas I was blind, now I see." [7]

A month later when the doctors again examined Madame Biré to see if she was still seeing with "dead" eyes they found that the phenomenon had ceased and that all traces of papillary atrophy had disappeared and that there were no longer any lesions. The healing was then considered to be complete.

Recently, two more Lourdes miracles have been reported by the press. In *Newsweek* of August 9, 1971, we have this story:

At the age of three, tiny Frances Burns was dying of cancer. She had already lost one kidney to abdominal blastoma and now the virulent disease was eating into her cheek and skull bones. Her body was skeleton thin, her skin candle-yellow and her head totally bald from unsuccessful drug treatments. "The blastoma had spread everywhere," recalls Dr. Stuart Mann, a surgeon at the Royal Hospital for Sick Children in Glasgow, Scotland. "The case had gone beyond surgery, and in this little girl there were all the signs of impending death."

As a last resort the child's desperate Roman Catholic mother decided to take Frances to the shrine of Our Lady of Lourdes

7 John 9:25.

in France, where the semiconscious little girl was carried to Mass and dunked in the shrine's miraculous water.

The article continues to report that on the third day after she had returned to Glasgow:

She sat up in bed and ate an orange. Almost overnight the bones in her skull began to grow again, and in time all traces of blastoma disappeared.

The *National Enquirer* of March 12, 1972, reports this case:

Mrs. Maria De Luca, forty-six, hit by an auto six years ago was left paralyzed. Numerous surgical operations and treatments proved useless.

Then one night last June she dreamed that the Madonna came to her and told her to go to the shrine of Lourdes, France. She left immobile, carried and pushed in a wheeled stretcher. Twelve days later she returned to her home. And she walked alone and unaided.

Countless numbers hail her cure as a miracle. The Vatican is investigating her case. Doctors who had pronounced her incurable are at a loss to explain her recovery.

The newspaper article shows pictures of Mrs. De Luca before and after her healing. In the "before" shot, she is lying on a wheeled stretcher. In the "after" shot, she is wearing a very chic pants suit and looking very fit indeed.

Asked by the *Enquirer* about her life now that she can walk, Mrs. De Luca said: "I spend my time doing what I can for the sick and answering hundreds of letters from people asking for faith. It is many months now since I was cured and it is as if I were never paralyzed. I have made a vow to the Madonna that I will go to Lourdes again next year—this time as a volunteer helper for the sick."

I was interested in her vow since it is reported that of the thousands of helpers at the shrine of Lourdes, stretcher-bearers, nurses, etc., a great many of them are people who have, themselves, been healed and have come back to help others.

### What Do All These Healings Have in Common?

There is no question in my mind that miraculous healings are taking place today. I have myself witnessed many of them. Not only are there miracles at Lourdes but in churches and healing groups of many different denominations. In our next chapter we will consider some of these different healing groups and see if we can discover a common denominator running through all of them.

### Man Is Not the Healer

You may be the instrument through which some person is able to receive his healing, but you are not the healer. I am not a healer. There is no power but of God.

The person whom you consider a healer, the practitioner or the minister who helps you, can be likened to the person who assists you in turning on the electric power in your new home. Suppose the contractor who builds your house takes you through the house showing you the various power outlets available to you. Here you will plug in your washing machine and your dryer. Another outlet will connect you with the power for your refrigerator, your freezer, your electric stove, your toaster, and all of the other appliances we take for granted today. "But," you say, "these outlets are dead. How do I turn on the main switch that will bring the power into the house?" So the contractor goes with you and shows you the master switch. You pull the switch and now there is power going to all of the different outlets, all that you will ever need and more. The contractor is not the power. The switch is not the power, but the connection has been made and now there is power in your house. Now, power is available to you, ready to fill the entire house with light, with energy for every service needed.

So it is with the Universal Mind Power. It has always been available, waiting to flow into our lives bringing health and abundance of every good thing, healing our bodies, our minds, and affairs. The so-called healer, like the contractor, knows that the Power is there. You might say that through his faith and understanding you are made aware of the Master Switch activated by your faith, your own belief that the Power does exist and is available to you. Once you have made your connection with the Power, it fills your mental house and you can draw upon It at will.

Just as you are able to use your vacuum cleaner, toast your bread in the morning, and find endless uses for the electric power in your house, so are there endless uses of the omnipotent Power, the great invisible Power that is available to us in every area of life. Healing, wholeness, energy, inspiration, supply, all of life's blessings are ours through the Power that is within us.

This is why any reputable practitioner or healer is quick to tell you, "I did nothing. The healing is of God." He means, "I simply introduced you to the omnipresent Power which is all in all, around you and through you and in you." It fills your house of consciousness. All Power belongs to God, but all that the Father hath is thine! How well Jesus understood this.

## Who Can Be Healed?

The important thing is that we do not have to get ourselves involved in symptoms or conditions, past physical history, or prognosis regarding the physical body. We are working with Spirit, and Spirit knows how to do all things. We do not have to change the body. The less we know about the body, the better off we are. The change must come in our belief about ourselves. The outer will always conform to the inner belief.

## Health Is Your Heritage

Good health belongs to you. It is your natural birthright. Holiness means wholeness, completeness. *Be ye therefor perfect, even as your Father which is in heaven is perfect.* You are created in the image and likeness of Divine Perfection. God Life within you is perfect. It knows neither sickness nor infirmity. It has never been contaminated. Nothing can be added to or taken away from God Life that is expressing through you. It is your life now. The perfect Life within you knows your needs as already fulfilled, for It can know no lack. That which has created you goes through this experience with you, moving on with you into all experiences throughout Eternity. It will never, never leave you. It is the individualization of the great Whole. It is what the Greeks called the

Microcosm in the Macrocosm. In the Christian teaching it is called the Christ of God. In Hinduism the individual Essence of God is called the Atman, ever moving toward Nirvana, the Universal Completeness. The idea that man is a perfect being for the expression of perfect Life is the basis of this life. That which is Perfect within us can never be extinguished. Fire cannot burn it; water cannot drown it; old age cannot deplete it. It is there ready to be recognized. For a time, it may seem to be suppressed but It can never become extinguished.

# THREE

## The Common Denominator

*Jesus said unto him, If thou canst believe, all things are possible to him that believeth.*—Mark 9:23

I am continually being asked, "What do you think about Kathryn Kuhlman and Oral Roberts? Do you really believe that they heal people?"

My answer is, "They, themselves, don't believe that *they* heal people. Yet, the healings take place. They will tell you that the omnipotent Power does the healing."

"But, what part do Oral Roberts and Kathryn Kuhlman play in the healings?" my questioners usually ask.

Before going any further, let us take a look at some of the healings. Perhaps then we can arrive at the common denominator.

A man attending one of my lectures urged me to go to one of Kathryn Kuhlman's healing meetings which was to be held the following week in San Diego and to explain to him what I thought took place. My wife and I did attend this meeting. It was necessary to get there two hours early to get a seat even though the meeting was held in San Diego's Civic Theater which seats thirty-four hundred people. There was a great feeling of expectancy. No one minded the wait at all, so great was the anticipation. The very air seemed electrically charged with faith among the people waiting in the crowd outside. When the doors finally opened an hour before the meeting (we had waited an hour outside), the theater was immediately filled to capacity. It was interesting because the publicity had been entirely by word of mouth. There had been very little advertising of the meeting and there was, in San Diego, no television or radio exposure of Kathryn Kuhlman's work at that time. For the next hour, the people around us buzzed with excitement at what was to come. And then Miss Kuhlman quietly walked out on the stage. My first impression was that she was a person of deep humility. She led the group assembled in singing "He Touched Me." It was a moving experience, first her clear voice starting the song and then the choir, gathered from many local churches, joined in and, finally, that huge theater was filled with the voices of thousands of people joining together. The deep sounds of the organ and the voices soared and filled the auditorium, and then Miss Kuhlman abruptly stopped the music. The healings began. They continued as fast as popcorn popping, first from the balcony, then from somewhere on the main floor. People kept coming forward and going onto the stage to attest to their healings. There was nothing planned, nothing staged. The people healed were filled with wonder and awe, and you could not help but believe that they were really healed. For two solid hours the healings continued; there must have been a hundred or more that evening. Miss Kuhlman herself became breathless as she announced the healings and talked to those healed. It all happened so fast. Many of the cases that evening had to do with arthritis, but people testified to healings of all kinds. Finally, at the end of the second hour, Miss Kuhlman quite suddenly brought the meeting to a close. "Oh, I haven't given my sermon! And I had such a good sermon prepared for you!" She, too, seemed awed at the number of healings that evening.

Do I believe that healings take place at Miss Kuhlman's meetings? I was there. I saw it with my own eyes. I heard it with my own ears. Yes, I believe that many were healed.

I used to watch Oral Roberts conduct his televized tent meetings. To me, the healings were most convincing. I consider Oral Roberts a man of deep convictions and strong faith.

### Faith Healing an Accepted Part of Life Today in the United States

Yes, spiritual healing has become quite reputable today. But it wasn't always so. In the nineteenth century when Christian Science pioneered this field, there was open hostility to the idea of mind over matter. Many actually thought that it was sacrilegious to even consider that the art of Spiritual Mind Healing had not ended with Jesus. I can remember in the early part of the twentieth century that a family of Christian Scientists on our block were considered to be strange people and were avoided by their more orthodox neighbors.

Yet the Christian Science movement, founded in 1866 by Mary Baker Eddy, has continued to grow and prosper. In her textbook, *Science and Health with Key to the Scrip-*

*tures,* Mrs. Eddy calls it "divine metaphysics . . . the scientific system of divine healing." Mrs. Eddy had not expected to found a distinct church or denomination. She hoped her discovery would be accepted by the existing churches and many of her early classes were conducted for medical doctors.

By 1950 there were over three thousand Churches of Christ Scientist throughout the world and their literature was available in many languages. Today I suppose the followers of Mary Baker Eddy number in the millions. I believe that much of this astounding growth is the result of the testimonial meetings conducted every Wednesday evening in the Christian Science churches. Have you ever attended one? There is an old saying, "If you haven't tried it, don't knock it!" When the meeting is open for testimonials of Christian Science healing, there are not one or two isolated cases, but there is hardly a lull during the half hour or so allowed. One by one, people quietly stand and give audible thanksgiving for marvelous healings they have experienced. I have several times attended these meetings and have been convinced of the honesty of those testifying to healings. It is my opinion that the many healing movements today owe Christian Science and its founder, Mary Baker Eddy, a great debt of gratitude for pioneering the rugged terrain of public opinion for more than a century until Spiritual Mind Healing has become not only respectable but, as Mrs. Eddy hoped, accepted by many churches and other groups today.

My wife attended college with a girl whose father was an M.D. and whose mother was a Christian Science practitioner. Connie asked her one day, "How does this work out? How do they get along?"

Her friend laughed. "They get along beautifully! My dad says, 'I cure the ones I can, and the ones I can't help, I send to mother!' "

Mrs. Eddy would be gratified today to see how many medical doctors recommend metaphysical and self-help books to their patients. Every day I receive orders for my books written on the prescription pads of doctors. I send my lessons on healing and related metaphysical studies to five or six hundred medical doctors each month. My literature is to be found in the waiting rooms of countless physicians. But, when you stop to think of it, why should it be strange for a doctor to combine every known means to help the people he has dedicated his life to help?

## A Strong Healing Movement in Japan

When I first heard that there were over three million people in Japan who are followers of Dr. Masaharu Taniguchi I was surprised, but not after I had read his book *You Can Heal Yourself.*[1] In this book he gives one account after another of healings of terminal cancer and other so-called incurable diseases. Dr. Taniguchi is the founder of a movement in Japan called Seicho-No-Ie. His monthly magazine, which many people in the United States receive, is also called *Seicho-No-Ie.*

The word Seicho-No-Ie means the whole universe. Here, *sei* and *cho* respectively means growth or extension in terms

[1] Masaharu Taniguchi, *You Can Heal Yourself* (Tokyo: Seicho-No-Ie Foundation, 1961).

of time and growth in terms of space; *no* is a connective that corresponds to of in English; and *ie* is a home. Therefore, together, it means literally the Home of Growth, and in a wide sense the Universe.

from: Siecho-No-Ie, published<br>monthly in Tokyo, Japan

I have heard Dr. Taniguchi lecture to large groups in this country, but I understand from those who have heard him in Japan that it is not unusual for ten thousand students to sit on the floor with their legs folded under them for two hours at a time to hear him. I personally do not doubt the authenticity of the healings that come through the vast work of Dr. Taniguchi.

## *What Do All These Healings Have in Common?*

Why have we spent so much time discussing ancient and modern accounts of healings? It is my desire in these first chapters of my book to present as many different approaches to Spiritual Mind Healing as I possibly can in order to pose the questions: What do all of these healings have in common? What is the common denominator, if any, of all spiritual healings?

Now, I should like to ask you, why should we doubt the ancient accounts of healing, the healings in Greece and Rome, the healings of Jesus and the Apostles, the healings at Lourdes, when so many miraculous healings take place today much nearer home?

Today Spiritual Mind Healing is practiced, and successfully, among many religious sects. There continue to be healings in Christian Science, Religious Science, Unity, Divine Science, and countless other metaphysical groups.

Brother Mandus from Blackpool, England, conducts healing missions all over the world. The Order of St. Luke's which was started in an Episcopal church in San Diego by the late Reverend Dr. John Gaynor Banks, together with his wife Ethel Tulloch Banks, conducts healing missions in churches of various denominations. Thousands attend these meetings and dramatic healings occur there.

But this is not all. There are healing meetings today in Pentacostal churches, Spiritualist churches, and churches of almost all denominations. In fact, modern day healings occur wherever the principle of Spiritual Mind Healing is accepted and practiced. The question we must ask ourselves is, *What is that principle?* Can anyone use it? Is it available to all regardless of creed or sect?

*The Common Denominator*

If the test of a true healing, as Paracelsus believed, is the recovery of the patient, if all of these people recover, regardless of the differences in terminology, regardless of the type of ritual or dramatic effects they employ at times, there must be something they have in common, some approach that they all share *that works.*

In the healings at the shrine of Aesculapius the results were obtained through the attitude that the statue of Aesculapius produced in the minds of the patients. The statue itself did not heal them, but in some way it opened the door to healing for them. Herein lies our clue.

In the healings at Lourdes the water itself does not have the power to cure. One of the fascinating things about the Lourdes story is that the water has been found to be highly polluted. In *The Miracle of Lourdes* Ruth Cranston discusses this strange phenomenon. The waters themselves contain no curative or medicinal properties whatever. However, she reports that a bacterial study of the water did reveal a remarkable fact. "The Medical Bureau, curious to learn why no infection resulted when one diseased patient after another was bathed in the same water, took samples from the baths and had them analyzed. The reports showed extreme pollution—streptococcus, staphylococcus, colibacillus, and all sorts of other germs. Yet, astonishingly, when guinea pigs were inoculated with this polluted water they remained perfectly healthy. At the same time, two out of three guinea pigs died when inoculated with water from the River Seine containing much the same bacilli." She says that at the end of the day, to prove their faith, the stretcher-bearers and nurses often dip a glass of water from the baths and drink it!

It wasn't the sliver of wood that healed people, for most of them were not really relics of the cross. It isn't the prayer cloth itself that changes the lives of those who believe in it.

Do you begin to see the silver thread that runs through all of these healings? Healing is an art. It is the art of turning the attention away from the condition and establishing in the mind a new concept—recognizing that this new concept will eliminate that which has been established from a false premise or belief.

The doctor may bind up the wound, but it is the divine Power within life itself that heals the patient. The practitioner or healer offers to you his conviction, his faith in the Almighty and Omnipresent Power of God. But if you do not accept his faith and make it your own, you will not receive a healing. Remember when Jesus went to his hometown? *He could there do no mighty work.*[2] He was just a hometown boy and they refused to believe that miracles could come through him. And he said, *A prophet is not without honour, but in his own country, and among his own kin, and in his own house.*[3]

The common denominator, the secret hidden in every healing, no matter what school of healing is consulted, is to be found in the statement made by Jesus, *It is done unto you as you believe.* Jesus had cast out demons and raised the dead, but in his own hometown he could do little because of their unbelief. It was his custom to ask those who came to him if they believed on him. *Though ye believe not me, believe the works.*[4] The greater their faith, the more spectacular the results.

When his followers came to him and bemoaned the fact that there were some cases that would not respond to their efforts to heal them, Jesus reproved them, *O ye of little faith!*[5] He regarded faith which he generally spoke of as *belief* as being essential to success in the art of healing, not only in the patient but in the healer, too. Thomson Jay Hudson comments on this:

If the Great Healer thus acknowledged a limitation of his powers, how can we, his humble followers, hope to transcend the immutable law of which he was governed.

It follows that, whatever may be the objective belief of the patient, if he will assume to have faith, actively or passively,

2 Mark 6:5.          3 Mark 6:4.
4 John 10:38.        5 Matthew 6:30.

the subjective mind will be controlled by the suggestion, and the desired result will follow.

The faith required for therapeutic purposes is a purely subjective faith, and is attainable upon the cessation of active opposition on the part of the objective mind.[6]

No, the Power was not in the sliver of wood; the Power was not in the statue of Aesculapius; the Power was not in the man Jesus; and, of course, the Power is not in the drugs people take. All Power belongs to God. The Almighty Power is the only Power. There is no other. *Thy faith hath made thee whole . . . of myself, I do nothing, the Father that dwelleth within me, he doeth the works.* The Power presses in upon us, waiting to express Itself through us. It is desire and belief that opens the door from within and lets the healing take place. The belief of the patient must unlock the door of his own doubt in order for him to receive the healing that was there waiting for him all the time. There are many avenues of healing but only one Healer. The doctor binds up the wound, yes, but the Life Process heals it through the ever present desire of Life to bring man back to his true state of spiritual Wholeness.

Therefore, if you believe in any avenue of healing enough to open your mind to receive the wholeness that is already yours, you have opened the door to That which was always there— *Behold, I stand at the door and knock.*[7] The various devices, whether they be prayer cloths, holy relics, holy water from the Jordan, or Grecian statues, only serve to lift the consciousness of the patient into a recep-

6 Hudson, *The Law of Psychic Phenomena.*          7 Revelations 3:20.

tive state so that he will give the Creative Process of Life a chance to heal him.

## A New Concept Is Needed

The body that we inhabit during this lifetime is not the dense thing that we imagine. It is a fluidic, ever changing instrument, entirely made of energy, the one Substance of Life. It is continually changing, recreating itself according to the mental pattern held up before it. Your body does not have a single cell that it contained a year ago. It may have the same marks and blemishes but if you remove them from the pattern they will begin to disappear. A person can be covered with warts one day and the next day have none. Where did they go? Did the dishrag buried under the tree have anything to do with it? Only your belief in the magic rite changed your mental concept.

Most people take the body far too seriously. The thing that is detrimental is the belief that the body cannot be changed because somebody has given a diagnosis concerning it. Tumors have disappeared into thin air. Those about to go on, having given up hope, have, through prayer, been raised up into a new vital experience. The infinite Intelligence within, having created this body, knows how to recreate it continually.

## Now Are We the Sons of God Made in the Image and Likeness of God

Let us know together that the Life that is God within us cannot be diminished by anyone's opinion of us. It cannot be diminished by anyone's diagnosis. Principle is perfect. It can never be altered or impaired.

All that God is, infinite and entire, is contained in this one moment. We don't have to make it happen. It already is. Moment by moment, we let It flow through us into Its own perfect expression.

Right now we are releasing all of the foolish thinking, the negative destructive thinking. We are emerging into a new fresh concept of ourselves, knowing that we are one with the Spirit of God within that is able to do all things.

Now are we the sons of God, made in the likeness of God. There is no separation. Divine Life within us reproduces Itself as perfect activity.

We thank Thee, Father, that Thou hearest us always. Before we called the answer was waiting. For this we are grateful. And so it is.

### It Is Up to You

Man can receive into his experience just as much of the Divine as he is willing to accept. Jesus accepted It so completely that he became synonymous with the Christ, God individualized in man, as man. He told us that the works that he did we could do also and even greater because he gave us his secret, *I go unto my Father*.[8] As we go to the Father within, the Source of all Life, we let the healing Power work through us.

[8] John 14:12.

# FOUR

## Spiritual Mind Treatment

*Verily, verily, I say unto you, He that believeth on me, the works that I do shall he do also; and greater works than these shall he do; because I go unto my Father.*—John 14:12

In this highly scientific age, the healing of the physical body is getting more attention than at any other time in the history of man. Billions of dollars are being spent annually to alleviate sickness. There are more hospitals, more medical facilities, more doctors, more technicians, and more and more people needing these services than ever before. Every time medical science eliminates the ravages of one disease, two more pop up to take its place. Is something being overlooked? Is there a better way? The answer is *yes*.

Two thousand years ago a man walked across the face of the earth who was able to heal people without drugs, doctors, or hospitals. The ministrations of this man lasted for only a few short years, three to be exact, but people are still talking about his works. The things that he did were called miracles because they were beyond human understanding. His name was Jesus. He was hailed by his followers as the Christ, the long-awaited Messiah.

## The Things That He Did We Can Do Also

Jesus himself said that the things that he did we could do also and even greater things. He gave us the key in one short phrase: *because I go unto my Father*. He selected and trained his twelve disciples. Then, it is recorded, he trained another seventy. He sent them out into the field and they, too, were successful in the work of healing. Clearly it was not meant to stop with them.

How did Jesus heal? He used scientific prayer. He turned away from the disturbing appearance and went unto the Father, the perfect Life within. Can we, too, use the Power that Jesus used? Yes; today we have available to us an understanding of scientific prayer through which miracles are wrought. Anyone who is willing to put aside all superstition, to put aside false beliefs and prejudices, to keep an open mind to receive instruction, can become a channel for healing. Healing through scientific prayer, the principles of which have existed down through the ages, has been rediscovered during the past century.

Healing is not confined to any one religious sect or group. Miraculous healings take place daily through the prayer work of many dedicated people.

## Everyone Is a Potential Healer

What I am going to say next will probably surprise you. We have all, at some time or other in our lives, been instruments for healing. While you possibly have not consciously engaged in scientific prayer for others, you quite probably have had uplifted states of consciousness that have had effective results. Every time you have had a recognition of good for another, every time you have eliminated negative thinking about another, every time you have identified another person with the God Power, you have had the rudimentary beginnings of a scientific prayer.

Who knows how many times the mind of man has entertained an inspired thought that has unwittingly blessed another—perhaps it was just a feeling of divine protection that was not even put into words, but it channeled the Power somewhere in the world and there was a lifting up of consciousness, a new awareness of Being with its corresponding improvement in the outer. Healing is not reserved for a certain favored few. You need not be a mystic nor one who has strange psychic experiences to be an instrument for healing. You need not see lights or hear voices. Each one of us is a potential *healer,* who lets the healing Power express through him.

There is nothing strange about healing. Spiritual Mind Healing is a very practical activity. There is nothing you can ever learn that will be of more value to you than the art and science of scientific prayer.

## Treatment Is Our Word for Scientific Prayer

Is there a prayer that is always answered? What does it mean to pray amiss? James said, *Ye ask, and receive not, because ye ask amiss.*[1] Have we asked amiss in the past? Can we learn now to pray aright and pray confidently, expecting to receive answers to our prayers?

Yes, I believe that there is a prayer that is always an-

1 James 4:3.

swered. We can learn to pray scientifically and confidently expect, if our prayers are motivated by Love, to have them answered.

The old way was to pray with the mind still occupied with the problem, a futile prayer that asked for strength to bear the burden. This prayer of petition sought to influence God to change the conditions that we had ignorantly brought upon ourselves. Scientific prayer, also called affirmative prayer, changes *us* that we may be receptive to the divine right action of God which is already established. The prayer of petition was to a God apart from man, a God afar off. Scientific prayer takes place in the One Mind and is directed to God within man. In order to eliminate confusion, I will call scientific prayer *spiritual mind treatment*. From now on every time we mention treatment we mean scientific prayer.

### Jesus Was the First Exponent of Scientific Prayer

Jesus taught and demonstrated that man had been given dominion over the things of this world through prayer. He healed the multitudes through scientific prayer, and when his disciples still did not understand, he cursed the fig tree to show them that all Power in heaven and in earth had been given to the son of man.

And in the morning, as they passed by, they saw the fig tree dried up from the roots.

And Peter calling to remembrance saith unto him, Master, behold, the fig tree which thou cursedst is withered away.

And Jesus answering saith unto them, Have faith in God.

For verily I say unto you, That whosoever shall say unto

this mountain, Be thou removed, and be thou cast into the sea; and shall not doubt in his heart, but shall believe that those things which he saith shall come to pass; he shall have whatsoever he saith.

Therefore, I say unto you, What things soever ye desire, when ye pray, believe that ye receive them, and ye shall have them.                                         Mark 11:20–24

What a powerful lesson! There was no limitation placed upon the use of the Power, a mountain could be removed and even something as seemingly negative as withering a fig tree was accomplished through the power of the word. It was *what things soever ye desire* with no limitation placed upon the desire. We live to prove his words today. We can have anything that we desire. It comes so fast sometimes that it startles us. If our desires are born in Love they bless us and all concerned. If they are not loving, we learn the hard way to make better choices next time.

### Ernest Holmes Defined Treatment

One of the clearest definitions of treatment ever given us is to be found in *The Science of Mind* by Ernest Holmes:

Treatment is the act, the art, and the science of inducing thought within the mentality of the one treating, which thought shall perceive that the body of the patient is a Divine, Spiritual, and Perfect Idea.[2]

2 Ernest Holmes, *The Science of Mind* (New York: Dodd, Mead & Co., 1946).

*Emmet Fox Had a Word for It*

Emmet Fox called treatment the Golden Key. He said that sicentific prayer would enable a person, sooner or later, to get himself, or anyone else, out of any difficulty on the face of the earth. He called scientific prayer the Golden Key to harmony and happiness. He suggested to the thousands of people who heard him lecture every week at Carnegie Hall in New York that they give it a fair trial, for it could be proved.' His inspired teaching was: God is omnipotent and man His image and likeness, thus man has dominion over all things. He told them that these words were to be taken literally and at their face value; that they were not the special prerogative of the mystic or the saint. For, he said, in scientific prayer it is God who works, and not you, and so your particular limitations or weaknesses are of no account in the process. He considered man the channel through which the divine action takes place, the treatment being the act of getting the human self out of the way. He promised that beginners would often get startling results at the first time of trying, for all that was absolutely essential was to have an open mind and sufficient faith to try the experiment. And, even more shocking, he held that one might hold any views on religion, or none, it made no difference.

I, personally, have found this to be true in my work with people. Sometimes beginners have the most dramatic results of all when they are first introduced to scientific prayer. Even agnostics have been healed and go away convinced that there is a Power in the Universe to which all things are possible.

As to the method of working in scientific prayer, Emmet Fox taught that it was simplicity itself. He put it this way:

All that you have to do is this: *Stop thinking about the difficulty, whatever it is, and think about God instead.* This is the complete rule, and if only you will do this, the trouble, whatever it is, will presently disappear. It makes no difference what kind of trouble it is. It may be a big thing or a little thing; it may concern health, finance, a law-suit, a quarrel, an accident, or anything else conceivable; but whatever it is, just stop thinking about it, and think about God instead—that is all you have to do.[3]

How simple it is and yet it works, if given a fair trial. "Do not try to form a picture of God, which is, of course, impossible," he warned. His method was to work by going over the attributes of God, the things that are known of God: God is Wisdom, Truth, inconceivable Love, present everywhere. The important thing was to stop thinking about the trouble and think about God instead, for if one were thinking about his trouble he could not, at the same time, be thinking about God. The secret was to become so absorbed in this consideration of spiritual values that, for a few moments at least, the problem was forgotten and then, he said, "you will presently find that you are safely and comfortably out of your difficulty."[4]

## Why Should We Ever Fail?

It all seems so simple. Why should we ever miss? We have only to turn our attention away from the problem

---

3 Emmet Fox, *Power Through Constructive Thinking* (New York: Harper & Row, 1940).
4 Ibid.

and think about God instead. We have to change our thought. This is where the difficulty comes in—we are not always able to turn our attention away from the problem and keep it focused on God. This is the reason that Mrs. Addington and I have spent a number of years in working out specific treatments for various needs designed to help the reader redirect his thinking into channels of right thinking and right expression.

Treatment is scientific prayer. It is an individual thought process whereby man's thinking is directed away from the need or problem and put in direct alignment with the divine Mind; thereby enabling him to receive his highest good.

"Our life is what our thoughts make it," said Marcus Aurelius. *As a man thinketh in his heart, so is he,* is another way of putting it. As long as man's attention is riveted on his problem or difficulty, he is going to reproduce into his experience more of the same. Through treatment his attention is focused upon the Infinite, and the result is that he then outpictures his new elevated thinking—infinite Intelligence, omnipotent Power and omnipresent Love. Through treatment man is given dominion. It is an open door to all that the Father hath. Through treatment, *all that the Father hath is thine.*

*My Father worketh hitherto and I work,* said Jesus. The Father's work is done, His creation is perfect. Treatment is man's work. Treatment transforms our thought into the pattern of our heart's desire. It is praying aright. It is the prayer that is always answered.[5]

## What Spiritual Mind Treatment Really Is

Perhaps if we understood what treatment really is, we would not feel so inadequate in its use. Treatment is a

[5] Jack and Cornelia Addington, *Your Needs Met*, Abundant Living Foundation, Box 100, San Diego, California, 1966.

clarification of the mind so that the divine perfect action of God can come through.

The nature of God is perfect Life. The words "in His name" in the Bible mean "in His perfect nature." The nature of spiritual man made in the image and likeness of God,[6] is also perfect. We are told, . . . *God hath made man upright; but they have sought out many inventions.*[7] Sickness and suffering are not God-ordained. They are the invention of mortal man. It is man who has blocked the flow of perfect Life by the negative thinking that he has allowed to control him. When we clear the mind of the debris of fear, envy, anxiety, and all of the other negative thoughts that have produced symptoms of illness, the wholeness of God shines through and we say that we have had a healing. In other words, we do not strive to change outer conditions through treatment but open the way for a restoration of the wholeness of mind that must show forth as wholeness of body.

When a person comes to you seeking spiritual help for himself, he is actually seeking a lift in consciousness. You do not have to make something happen. You do not have to change his conditions. All you have to do is raise your consciousness by knowing the Truth about him. Your job is to know the Truth of Being. Know that God is all in all, over all, and through all. Know that God is the only Cause and Creator; that God is the only Power, and that anything that would deny this Power is therefore a lie. You do not have to convince him of this Truth. As you know it for him, he will be lifted in consciousness. This is what

6 Genesis 1:26.                                               7 Ecclesiastes 7:29.

Jesus meant when he said, *And I, if I be lifted up from the earth, will draw all men unto me.*[8]

## Three Steps in Spiritual Mind Treatment

There are three all-important steps in treatment. I call them the three *R*'s of treatment. They are:

1. Recognition
2. Realization
3. Release

## Recognition Is the First Step in Treatment

The first thing that the scientist discovered when he began to study the sun was that the sun is always there. It made no difference what the appearances were. In the midst of a tornado, in the midst of storm or darkness, the sun is always there. The first step in treatment is the recognition that God is. The omnipresence of God assures us that wherever we may be, God is always there. The omnipotence of God assures us that God is all Power. *Behold, I am the Lord, the God of all flesh: is there any thing too hard for me?* [9] We may become almost analytical at this stage in meditating on what God is. *There is no power but of God.*[10] Use Bible verses, hymns, or poems, anything that cuts through the clouds of human belief to the omnipresent Truth about God. God is omniscient, all-knowing, and this means that no problem can stand in the way. The

8 John 12:32.　　　　　　　　　9 Jeremiah 32:27.
10 Romans 13:1.

three *omni's* are always a good place to start in step number one: omnipotence, omniscience, omnipresence. Any attributes of God that help to give you a recognition of God—Life, Love, Wisdom, Power, Goodness, Beauty, Peace—are food for meditation. It is highly important in this first step that you have a true concept of God. The other two steps depend upon it.

### Realization Is the Second Step in Treatment

The second step is realization or making God real in *your* life. You can sit all day, like the Hindus, and recognize God, but if you do not identify yourself with God you have nothing. Take the great swami who sat in the bliss of samadhi, meditating day and night about God while his body was wasting away with cancer. He did not identify the whole self with the God Life—spirit, mind, *and body.* If God is all in all, we cannot say this is of God and this is not of God. It is all of the essence of God and we must realize that the omnipresent Goodness of God is translated into human experience; that no matter how serious the problem is, God, Infinite, all-knowing Intelligence, has a perfect answer. We must know that we cannot become separated from the Omnipresence there. Whenever a problem begins to creep back into the mind through the doorway of fear and doubt, we must push the problem out and close the door upon it by realizing, "God is the only Power in my life now." Realization means unification with God and acceptance of the attributes of God in our own lives and affairs. It is not going off into some sort of fantasy. It is an acceptance of divine Omnipresence here and now.

Jesus understood the importance of realization and used it in his own prayers. *I and my Father are one. For as the Father hath life in himself; so hath he given to the Son to have life in himself. Glorify thou me with thine own self with the glory which I had with thee before the world was.*[11]

## The Third Step Is Release

A young man remarked to me, "Until I learned the true meaning of release, I never received an answer to my prayers. I read the story of Jesus and the centurion over and over—of how the centurion would order the soldiers and they would do exactly as they were ordered. The centurion trusted them to do what he told them to do. The centurion expected Jesus to trust God to heal his servant. That is why Jesus said, *Such faith I have not seen in all Israel.*

This young man saw that once we turn to God, we have to trust God, act as though God has already answered our prayers, even though the evidence has not yet appeared.

The Christ awareness knows: *I speak not of myself: but the Father that dwelleth in me, he doeth the works.* Release is letting go and letting God. Release is being so sure that everything is being done that you can give thanks even before the manifestation appears. As Jesus said before the tomb of Lazarus, *Father I thank thee that thou*

11 John 10:30; 5:26; 17:5.

*hast heard me. And I knew that thou hearest me always.*[12] Release is the final step in getting the limited self out of the way so that the Almighty Power can come through. Release is the final and total act of surrender.

## How One Family Used Spiritual Mind Treatment

Here is an example of how a family used spiritual mind treatment effectively. Their only son had run away from home at the age of fifteen. At first the parents were beside themselves with fear and worry. And then they remembered that there was something that they could do. They did not have to walk the floor and wring their hands, there was something concrete and of proven effectiveness to do. They used spiritual mind treatment—scientific prayer.

They mentally disciplined themselves to turn away from all thought of the boy being hungry or influenced by evil companions. How were they able to do this? By recognizing that God is everywhere present, they were able to take the second step and realize that wherever that boy was, God was there, that God knew how to take care of him. Again and again they affirmed: "God is living through our son. Divine Wisdom lives through him. Divine Love surrounds him and keeps him. Divine Intelligence motivates and directs him."

You see, the recognition was that God is omnipresent. The realization came when God became very real in this experience. Then they could accept the fact that this boy could never become separated from God.

At last they were able to release him completely into

12 John 11:41, 42.

God's loving care. They told me that they finally reached the point where they could say: "If God is where our boy is, if God lives through our son, if divine Intelligence directs and guides him, then what is there to worry about? Why shouldn't we release the boy to God?"

The father and mother came to recognize the Presence of God and the oneness of their son with that Presence and when It became real to them, they were able to trust their son to God. At last they found peace of mind. They were no longer fearful.

In a few weeks the family heard from him. He telephoned from a distant city. He said that he had been very well treated, that everywhere he went people were kind and helpful. The Love that had been realized in prayer became Love experienced by him. This only made the boy miss his family more. He began to think about the love in his own home. Now he was eager to return to his family. They wired the money for his fare home and there was a very happy reconciliation. This is an example of how treatment can be used effectively. It does not matter what the problem happens to be—a problem within a family such as this one, a physical healing, overcoming a sense of lack—treatment is equally effective in each of these areas.

## What Is the Difference Between Scientific Treatment and Random Prayer?

Sometimes people question whether it is right and proper to follow a formula for prayer. "Should not prayer be purely inspirational?" they ask. The reason for treatment is obvious. Have you ever tried to pray when you did not feel on the beam spiritually? Have you ever faced a crisis such as that of the family whose son ran away, and found that your prayers not only lacked the conviction of faith but were empty words? Treatment gives you something you can fall back on in any emergency. Before you have completed the first step you should be getting yourself back in the spiritual groove where your words are no longer empty. Treatment quiets the mind and restores the faith that moves mountains, until the treatment grows and becomes more inspired as it develops. Treatment is available to us when we need it most. The old way meant we had to wait until we were on the mountain tops of consciousness before we could believe. Spiritual mind treatment builds our faith and lifts us out of the valleys.

Perhaps we can better understand treatment by taking a look backward at the way we used to pray.

## The Prayer of Petition

What about the prayer of petition? The prayer of petition is petitioning a Higher Power to grant a request. The prayer of petition is the usual orthodox prayer. There are many approaches and many variations, but you could hardly call this prayer scientific. There is, to be sure, a recognition of the higher Power, but where there is a petition, the concentration is usually on that petition and great attention is given to the problem or difficulty.

There is also apt to be a feeling of separation between the unworthy petitioner and the far-off Grantor. In treatment, there is no feeling of separation. Through step number two, we discover that the Father and son are one. *Son, thou art ever with me, and all that I have is thine.*[13] There is no separation between Creator and creation. We do not have to go to some power apart from us to please or woo this Power, trying to get its attention and favor. There is no need to use certain words or forms or positions of prayer. The Power comes into treatment through a realization of the existence of perfect unity, perfect oneness expressing in and through every part of life. This happens where there is the elimination of fear, worry, and anxiety so that the Light can come through. . . . *God is Light, and in him is no darkness at all.*[14] Spiritual mind treatment is based on this Truth. God is Truth and in Him is no negation at all. Just as the sun is still there even when we cannot see it, the Light of Truth endures. Treatment makes us aware of the Truth that sets us free. It brings us the specific truth that we need to free us from sense of lack and separateness. It brings us the awareness of Love which is the unifying substance of all Life tying us together in harmony and oneness.

By contrast, the prayer of petition is a futile prayer. It is futile because at the very beginning it sets up a sense of separation.

## The Prayer of Intervention

What is the prayer of intervention? The prayer of intervention came about very simply. Down through the ages, man believed that he was a worm of the dust. He felt separated from God, far removed from the Deity. It has

---

13 Luke 15:31.                                    14 I John 1:5.

been difficult for man to think of himself as being one with That which created him.

The prayer of intervention stems from a belief that God is over there; I am over here. God won't listen to me because I don't have enough authority, not enough influence. I must therefore contact an intervener, a go-between, one who has influence with God and who is able to communicate also with this lesser being, man. So man talks to the intercessor and the intercessor talks to God. This intercessor, of course, has to be some very special person supposed to have a direct line to God, such as a priest or minister, one who, you might say, has special privileges in heaven. An example of intercessory prayer is prayer to the saints. To pray to the saints to intercede for us is actually the same thing as asking a minister or practitioner to pray for you, an admission that we have no confidence in our own prayers and need someone whom we think is more worthy as a go-between.

I suppose this all started because Jesus said, *No man cometh unto the Father, but by me.*[15] Here again he was misunderstood. He so completely identified himself as the Christ that he spoke as the Christ, he *thought it not robbery to be equal with God.*[16] He referred to the indwelling Presence. No man cometh unto the Father but by the doorway of the Christ Consciousness. No man cometh unto the Omnipotent but through that mind *which was also in Christ Jesus,*[17] that spirit within which is one with the Spirit of God. He understood so completely that we were

[15] John 14:6.
[16] Philippians 2:6.
[17] Philippians 2:5.

not to bow down and put God over there, or think that we must talk *at* God. No, we were to go through the doorway of the Christ mind, that mind that is one with God. He was talking about the second step in scientific prayer, the unification of the son of God with his divine Source. The prayers of Jesus were truly scientific and this is why they were answered. This is why, if we have *that mind in us which was also in Christ Jesus,* we do not need an intercessor. The Christ within is our doorway, our contact with the Almighty Power.

### Spriritual Mind Treatment—A Way of Life

Of all the gifts that have been given to us as sons of God, there is none more awe-inspiring and none more wonderful than the gift of treatment. *It is your Father's good pleasure to give you the kingdom.*[18] Through treatment we are given the Golden Key to the kingdom. We discover that God is everywhere present, all Power, all Intelligence. God is consciously available to us. We have been given the right to choose whether we wish to live in chaos and confusion or to have our minds centered in peace. We can choose whether conditions of disease and disorder be allowed to control our lives or whether we take dominion through treatment.

The common thinking about prayer is that it is to be used only in an emergency or that it is a ritual indulged in only at certain special times in church or other sacred places. You will see, however, that through treatment, one can follow the admonition of Paul and pray without ceas-

18 Luke 12:32.

ing, and the admonition of Jesus that one should pray and not faint. As we begin to understand more about treatment, we see that it becomes more of a way of life and not a method of attaining temporary help or the peace that may come from following a daily ritual.

Let us review the three R's of treatment: *recognition, realization,* and *release.* The Golden Key is to turn away from the apparent condition, circumstance, or limitation and recognize the presence of God. Next, we realize our oneness with God by knowing that God lives through us. We now realize that the condition, circumstance, or problem has no power over us and that the only power is God living through us. We realize further that God translates Himself through us into perfect health, abundant supply, and perfect right action in our affairs. We know that all that needs to be done is being done in perfect order and at the right and perfect time. So we release the condition, circumstance, or problem, and continue to give our attention to the infinite and perfect Presence of God.

## Some Learn by Using Written Treatments

Sometimes it is helpful to learn to use treatment by following treatments that have been written by those who understand how to use the Principle. At the end of this and each following chapter you will find an example of spiritual mind treatment given in the first person in order to make it personal to you.[19]

[19] Treatments at end of chapters from *Your Needs Met* by Jack and Cornelia Addington, Abundant Living Foundation, Box 100, San Diego, California, 92138.

Words, of themselves, are empty, meaningless symbols. Their only value is the understanding that they bring to the reader, the deep feeling which they convey to the heart. Any prayer or meditation repeated over and over without meaning is an empty talisman, as superstitious a pastime as the wearing of a primitive charm.

*But when ye pray, use not vain repetitions, as the heathen do: for they think that they shall be heard for their much speaking.* Matthew 6:7

The mere reading of the words will accomplish nothing. It is suggested that you read these spiritual mind treatments over several times slowly, meditate on them until you can assimilate them, make them your own. In the Silence that follows, the Spirit of Truth will seem to speak to you.

### A SPIRITUAL MIND TREATMENT FOR YOU

*And when ye stand praying, forgive, if ye have aught against any; that your Father also which is in heaven may forgive you.*
—Mark 11:25

Turning from the problems and cares of the day, I now consciously accept the Truth about God and myself. I know that God is the only Power and the only Presence. I know that I am the expression of God and that all the Father hath is mine. I am a divine, perfect, spiritual being, forever one with my Source. Turning from problems, I listen in the Silence for God's perfect answers. Turning from confusion, I accept the Peace that passeth all understanding. I let the perfect Life of God live through me.

I now release all those who have ever hurt or offended me. I forgive them completely. I forgive myself for the mistakes of the past. Releasing others, I am released. Love is the answer to my every need.

All that I need or desire is right within me. In this moment of Silence the work is done. The Spirit within me is the Substance of all my desires. I joyously and thankfully accept the good I desire for myself and the good I desire for others. That which I realize in the invisible becomes manifest in my world. Forgiveness has opened the door to divine right action in my life.

And so it is.[20]

20 So be it: the literal meaning of Amen.

# FIVE

## Jesus Taught Scientific Prayer

*After this manner therefore pray ye.*

—Matthew 6:9

Many people do not pray because they do not know how to pray. One time I spoke on scientific prayer to a group of ministers from various denominations, members of a ministerial association. I soon realized that they were intensely interested in what I had to say. After the lecture one of the men came to me and confided that he had lately been omitting the pastoral prayer from his Sunday service and that no one had missed it. After an awkward pause, he confessed that he didn't know how to pray. I couldn't believe my ears. This was the minister of one of the largest churches in the city, a church that had several thousand members, telling me that he would like to attend my classes on scientific prayer because he did not know how to pray and had come to the point where he did not even pray in his Sunday service.

*Is There a Perfect Prayer?*

Let's go back to the man who not only knew how to pray effectively, but went apart and prayed for days at a time. I'm speaking of Jesus, who had quite a bit to say about how to pray. He gave us the Lord's prayer which is used in all Christian churches today, a prayer that lives because it is scientifically sound. It covers everything, as we shall see when we analyze it a little later. But Jesus was not content to give us a model prayer; he gave us quite a bit of instruction about praying in general.

Jesus himself, like all Hebrew boys, a good student of the Old Testament, had made a study of scientific prayer. One of the great prayers of all time is to be found in I Chronicles. Note the similarity to the Lord's Prayer.

Wherefore David blessed the Lord before all the congregation: and David said, Blessed be thou, Lord God of Israel our father, for ever and ever. Thine, O Lord, is the greatness, and the power, and the glory, and the victory, and the majesty: for all that is in the heaven and in the earth is thine; thine is the kingdom, O Lord, and thou art exalted as head above all. Both riches and honour come of thee, and thou reignest over all; and in thine hand is power and might; and in thine hand it is to make great, and to give strength unto all. Now therefore, our God, we thank thee, and praise thy glorious name. —I Chronicles 29:10–13

What a beautiful prayer! If ever there was a scientific prayer this is it. It combines recognition of the power and might of God with realization—*our* Father, *our* God—and concludes with release—*now therefore, our God, we thank thee.* So great is the recognition and realization of the Almighty Power here that David, who portrays the Christ Consciousness in the Old Testament, gives thanks for the answers that he has already accepted in complete faith. Are riches and honor needed? Then they are available for they *come of thee.* Do we need power and might, greatness and strength? Then, they, too, are at hand, *in thine hand,* and so we give thanks *and praise thy glorious name.*

## How Often Should We Pray?

Jesus said that *men ought always to pray and not to faint.* And then he illustrated this with a parable about a widow who continued to approach a very stern and independent judge asking him to avenge her of her enemies and the unjust judge decided to answer her request because she was so persistent. The parable clearly pointed out that we should persist in our prayer work and not give up.

And he spake a parable unto them to this end, that men ought always to pray, and not to faint;

Saying, There was in a city a judge, which feared not God, neither regarded man:

And there was a widow in that city; and she came unto him, saying, Avenge me of mine adversary.

And he would not for a while: but afterward he said within himself, Though I fear not God, nor regard man;

Yet because this widow troubleth me, I will avenge her, lest by her continual coming she weary me.

And the Lord said, Hear what the unjust judge saith.

And shall not God avenge his own elect, which cry day and night unto him, though he bear long with them?

I tell you that he will avenge them speedily. Nevertheless when the Son of man cometh, shall he find faith on earth?

Luke 18:1–8

Jesus admonished us to persist in prayer without fainting. What does faint mean? Webster's International Dictionary defines faint: To remain inactive instead of acting; to be sluggish or lazy; wanting in courage, spirit or energy; timorous; dejected; depressed; half-hearted. To faint is to sink into dejection; to lose courage or spirit; to become depressed or despondent. To be fainthearted is to be wanting in courage; depressed by fear; easily discouraged or frightened. "Faint heart ne'er won fair lady" says the old proverb. Nor does faint heart know answered prayer, I might add. Why do we become fainthearted? Because we are fearful, anxious, troubled. Often our prayers are half-hearted because we lack faith; we don't really believe that they are going to be answered anyway.

Praying without fainting is a continual turning to the power and wisdom of God right within us for direction and inspiration. It is a continual recognition that the power and wisdom of God within can and will meet every circumstance, situation, condition, or need that may arise in our day-to-day living. It is a realization of the constant availability of the power and wisdom of God; and a releasing of the responsibilities of the moment to the power and wisdom of God within. How can we say that one moment is God's moment and the next moment is not God's moment? God is in every moment. Faith in God is trusting in the power and widom of God within, irrespective of outer conditions and circumstances.

In a long-distance telephone conversation with a woman this morning, she told me, "Everything worked out wonderfully for Jane even though she went through many dark hours." Jane and others had been praying during those dark hours and there were those who questioned the validity and the effectiveness of prayer because things were not turning out the way they thought they should. In the end "everything worked out wonderfully."

Prayer is the inner action of the Spirit through the direction of mind. *All things work together for good to them that love God.*[1] Loving God above all else, moment by moment, is persisting in scientific prayer as Jesus taught.

## How Are We to Pray?

The parable of the Pharisee and the Publican brings out the idea that the most effective prayer work is done in deep humility. We are not to tell God how great we are but lean heavily on His Power.

Two men went up into the temple to pray; the one a Pharisee, and the other a publican.

The Pharisee stood and prayed thus with himself, God, I thank thee, that I am not as other men are, extortioners, unjust, adulterers, or even as this publican.

I fast twice in the week, I give tithes of all that I possess.

And the publican, standing afar off, would not lift up so much as his eyes unto heaven, but smote upon his breast, saying, God be merciful to me a sinner.

I tell you, this man went down to his house justified rather than the other: for every one that exalteth himself shall be abased; and he that humbleth himself shall be exalted.

Luke 18:10–14

A young minister was invited to speak in a large church by an older and more experienced minister. This young

[1] Romans 8:28.

man thought that here was an opportunity to really show how good he was and why possibly that church needed him for their minister. The older minister was noted for being a very loving man but without glamor or eloquent speech.

When the great day arrived, the two ministers went down and sat in the first row. The younger man had spent hours grooming himself perfectly and going over word for word all of the eloquent and impressive speech with which he planned to astound the congregation. At last the time came for him to speak. Stepping into the pulpit with a jaunty and confident air, he looked out on the sea of faces and all of a sudden his mind went blank. His prepared speech just wasn't there. Nothing was there. As he stood there, he began to deflate like a punctured balloon. After a couple of minutes of just standing there, dejectedly and slowly he walked back to his seat and sat down beside his colleague. The older man whispered to him, "If you had gone up as you came down, you would have come down as you went up."

*Pride goeth before destruction and a haughty spirit before a fall.*[2] Sincerity and honesty are essential ingredients of unification with the Spirit of Truth within. As one unifies with Spirit, the Spirit becomes real in his experience and this is true realization.

Jesus loved the rich young man but the rich young man put his possessions ahead of the love of God. The Pharisee in the parable placed the letter ahead of the Spirit of Truth. God will not be mocked. Divine Intelligence knows the intentions of our heart regardless of what we say with our lips or do with our hands.

2 Proverbs 16:18.

Humility does not mean to belittle or demean the self but to put God first in our lives.

## Where Should We Pray

Jesus said that prayer was a very private matter, not a matter of being heard of men but of communing with the Father in secret.

And when thou prayest, thou shall not be as the hypocrites are: for they love to pray standing in the synagogues and in the corners of the streets, that they may be seen of men. Verily I say unto you, They have their reward. But thou, when thou prayest, enter into thy closet, and when thou hast shut the door, pray to thy Father which is in secret; and thy Father which seeth in secret shall reward thee openly.—Matthew 6:5,6

Today we are inclined to think of a closet as a tiny room for clothes, a little wardrobe without any windows or air. This would be an unlikely place to pray.

At the time of Jesus, a closet meant a room for privacy such as a potentate's private chamber for counsel and household devotions. The dictionary carries it a step further, saying that a closet is a place of seclusion or privacy, without any distinction as to dimensions or size in any way whatsoever.

In the true sense we carry our closet with us wherever we go. We can be private even though we are in a crowd. We can be private at any moment of the day by declaring ourselves in a state of privacy. One can pray at any time *in his closet,* the closet of his mind, and there he will find God waiting for him.

By entering into the closet, we close the door on conditions, limitations and appearances. There in communion with the Absolute, we let our needs be known. Having sought and found our spiritual Source, we are able to let go of the striving and contention, the confused thinking of the past or of the moment. We do not have to make something happen. Why? Because the *Father which seeth in secret shall reward thee openly.*

Where does the Bible tell us Jesus prayed? *He departed into a mountain to pray; departed into a solitary place and there prayed; he withdrew himself into the wilderness and prayed; continued all night in prayer.*[3]

When we understand the inner meaning of these references, we see that these so-called places actually refer to states of consciousness. The wilderness is the wilderness of unenlightened thought. It is when we are in the wilderness that we need most to pray. In other words, we need to pray for inspiration. To go up into a mountain means to lift one's thinking to a high state of spiritual consciousness. To go into a solitary place means to remove oneself from the confusion and the chaotic thinking of the world. Throughout the Bible, the night signifies a dark period in man's consciousness or a state of ignorance. The Bible tells us to pray through the night until the light comes. This means to pray through the dark period in consciousness until enlightment or spiritual awareness comes.

In other words, Jesus clearly stated and showed that we are to pray through every situation and not just wait until we happen to be inspired to pray or to wait until we get into religious surroundings such as a church to pray.

3 Matthew 6:26;1:35; Luke 6:12.

### No Condition Placed Upon Our Desires, No Limitation on the Power

How often we hear people say, "I didn't think that I should bother God with my little problem." My answer is, "If it is important to you, it is important to God." Others cringe at the thought of praying for money or things. Piously, they repeat to me, "Money is the root of all evil." But the Bible doesn't say that. The scripture says: *For the love of money is the root of all evil.*[4] It is only when we worship money, putting it ahead of the Source of all good that we get into trouble. Let's see what Jesus had to say about praying for our needs.

Therefore I say unto you, What things soever ye desire, when ye pray, believe that ye receive them, and ye shall have them.—Mark 11:24

*What things soever* he said with no qualifications, no conditions. He didn't say, "Be sure that you just pray for spiritual understanding" when the immediate need is a bag of groceries. No, it was *what things soever.* The only admonition was to *believe that ye receive them.* It was *ask and it shall be given you, seek and ye shall find; . . . for everyone that asketh receiveth.* It was clearly implied that we ask of God the Source of all.

And he said unto them, Which of you shall have a friend, and shall go unto him at midnight, and say unto him, Friend, lend me three loaves;

For a friend of mine in his journey is come to me, and I have nothing to set before him?

And he from within shall answer and say, Trouble me not:

4 I Timothy 6:10.

the door is now shut, and my children are with me in bed; I cannot rise and give thee.

I say unto you, Though he will not rise and give him, because he is his friend, yet because of his importunity he will rise and give him as many as he needeth.

And I say unto you, Ask, and it shall be given you; seek, and ye shall find; knock, and it shall be opened unto you.

For every one that asketh receiveth; and he that seeketh findeth; and to him that knocketh it shall be opened.

If a son shall ask bread of any of you that is a father, will he give him a stone? or if he ask a fish, will he for a fish give him a serpent?

Or if he shall ask an egg, will he offer him a scorpion?

If ye then, being evil, know how to give good gifts unto your children: how much more shall your heavenly Father give the Holy Spirit to them that ask him?

Luke 11:5–13

## He Warned Against Empty Words and Much Speaking

Prayer, to Jesus, was not a lot of pretty words strung together, nor did he think it was necessary to tell God our troubles. So, before he gave to the people the model prayer, the Lord's prayer, the prayer that acts upon the heart of the one praying, he paved the way by telling them:

But when ye pray, use no vain repetitions, as the heathen do: for they think that they shall be heard for their much speaking. Be not ye therefore like unto them: for your Father knoweth what things ye have need of, before ye ask him.

—Matthew 6:7, 8

## The Practice of the Presence Was a Way of Life With Jesus

Jesus understood scientific prayer as no other man before him or since. He was able to speak his word and the healings were instantaneous. Through constant communion with the Spirit within, he was able to build his spiritual consciousness so that when a person touched the hem of his garment in faith, the healing took place. This man who prayed often and effectively did not tell his troubles to God. He recognized the Power and Presence of the Almighty Power and was so sure that he was heard of God that he gave thanks before the healing appeared. So sure was he that *I and my Father are one* that it was not necessary for him to go through a lengthy process of conditioning his mind to accept this awareness. He tried to share this awareness with us. *I am the light of the world,* he said, *he that followeth me . . . shall have the light of life.*[5] But here is where most people miss his message. He did not set himself apart from us for he also said, *Ye are the light of the world.*[6]

When we are able to accept the Christ Consciousness, knowing that we are never apart from the Father, feeling the Love of God with us and around us, accepting the Light (divine Illumination) in all that we do, we, too, shall not need to consciously achieve that state of consciousness where others shall touch the hem of our garment (our awareness) and be healed, for we shall be one with it.

[5] John 8:12.                                  [6] Matthew 5:14.

*Seek Ye First the Kingdom of God*

It was true two thousand years ago and it is true today. *Seek ye first the kingdom of God, and his righteousness; and all these things shall be added unto you.*[7] How does one seek the kingdom of God? We say it so glibly. What is the kingdom, anyway? The kingdom is that center of divine Power within, the dominion that comes when we are in tune with the divine Power. It is turning to that center of Peace and Love and Truth within, which men call God. *Be still and know that I am God* (within you).[8] It is through treatment (scientific prayer) that we seek the kingdom.

The thing to remember is that the alcoholic does not have to be an alcoholic, the sick person does not have to stay sick, the poor person does not have to stay poor, the sad person does not have to stay sad. There is a healing for everyone who is willing to seek the kingdom within.

Seeking the kingdom of God is the Golden Key that we referred to earlier. It is turning away from the conditions and realizing that all of the attributes of God are right where we are. Right where we are is infinite Intelligence, all-Power, divine Love, Peace, and perfect right action. The most thrilling thing that can ever happen to a person is to realize that God, the living Presence, is right within and can be experienced. The only reason that people become ill and stay ill is because they get off the track through fear, anxiety, resentment, and stress of all kinds. They keep the attention focused on the wrong thinking and subsequent conditions.

[7] Matthew 6:33.                    [8] Psalms 46:10.

One time I was asked to speak at an Alcoholics Anonymous meeting. I was very interested in what the various speakers had to say as one by one they testified how they had been able to stay dry. There are twelve steps in the A.A. program. The first three steps are:

1. We admitted we were powerless over alcohol—that our lives had become unmanageable.
2. Came to believe that a Power greater than ourselves could restore us to sanity.
3. Made a decision to turn our will and our lives over to the care of God *as we understood Him.*

Isn't that what we are talking about? It doesn't matter what form of sickness our false thinking has led us into, the first thing we have to do is turn our will and our lives over to the care of God *as we understand Him.* This is turning to the kingdom of God within. I remember one of the A.A. people used a cliché that evening that has stuck with me. He said, "There's only one way out: Quit your stinkin thinkin!"

## Teach Us to Pray

And it came to pass, that, as he was praying in a certain place, when he ceased, one of his disciples said unto him, Lord, teach us to pray, as John also taught his disciples.

—Luke 11:1

And Jesus responded by giving them that all inclusive prayer which, for two thousand years, has continued to be used by those who followed his teaching. There are many creeds among his followers but they all accept the Lord's Prayer:

After this manner therefore pray ye: *Our Father which art in heaven, Hallowed be thy name.*

*Thy kingdom come. Thy will be done in earth, as it is in heaven.*

*Give us this day our daily bread.*

*And forgive us our debts, as we forgive our debtors.*

*And lead us not into temptation, but deliver us from evil: For thine is the kingdom, and the power, and the glory, for ever. Amen.*—Matthew 6:9–13

### The Prayer That Lives for Everyone

It is said that the daughter of an atheist, who herself disclaimed any faith in prayer, told a friend that in an old German book she had come across a prayer that she could not forget despite her unbelief in prayer. She then remarked, "If a God exists who inspired that prayer I could believe in Him!"

This intrigued her friend who asked her if she could tell her more about the prayer. The girl who thought of herself as an atheist then slowly repeated the Lord's Prayer in German.

It seems strange to us that anyone could be unaware of the prayer that ties all Christianity together. But, we are not amazed that it moved her as it did. This prayer is considered the loftiest instrument of worship. It is also the most valid conception of man's relationship to God and the most beautiful and inspiring prayer known to man.

Did you notice how much it resembles the prayer of David? Only out of great illumination could these two great prayers have been born. That they have endured for thousands of years proves it.

*Recognition, Realization, Release—The Three Steps Are There*

The Lord's Prayer not only establishes the Presence of God within us and within all of Life, but lifts us to a realization of our oneness with Life.

*Scientific Prayer Is Always in the Present Tense*

It is said that the Lord's Prayer was originally given in the present tense. In the Aramaic, which is Jesus' native tongue, there is no past nor future tense. All prayers should be in the present tense. In the mind of God there is no yesterday and no tomorrow, only the Eternal Now. Being is a verb, not a noun. God is Being, continually unfolding His Creation. The recognition of God must be now and the realization of His Life being lived through us must be now. Tomorrow is always tomorrow for tomorrow never comes. The only time we can ever experience is now. Therefore, we have: *Thy kingdom come,* now. The allness of God accepted, now. Thy kingdom is come for Thou art changeless and eternal.

Why should we command God to do what He has already done? Instead of demanding: *Give us this day our daily bread,* try interpreting the words this way: *Thou givest us this day our daily bread, now.* For an interesting experiment try the Lord's Prayer entirely in the present tense. Isn't it a lot more meaningful?

Our Father which art in heaven,
Hallowed is Thy name.

Thy kingdom is come; Thy will is done on earth
as it is in heaven.
Thou givest us this day our daily bread:
Thou forgivest us our trespasses as we forgive
those who trespass against us.
Thou leadest us not into temptation but dost
deliver us from all evil:
For thine is the kingdom, and the power, and
the glory, for ever. Amen.[9]

## Our Father

Although Jesus generally referred to the Deity as Father,
he did not originate the term. We find God spoken of as
Father in the Old Testament, meaning Source, Inventor,
Creator, Ancestor. David called God *Father* in the Psalms:
*He shall cry unto me, Thou art my Father, my God, and
the rock of my salvation.*[10] And, again in I Chronicles in
the prayer so similar to the Lord's prayer: *Blessed be thou,
Lord God of Israel our father, for ever and ever.*[11] To the
Hebrew not only did the word "father" stand for the
orginator who gave life to his offspring, even his own life
and characteristics—*in his image and likeness*—but to the
Hebrew the father was a patriarch with absolute authority
over his subjects. The word in the Hebrew is *Ab* and the
prefix *Ab* in many Hebrew names is connected with the
term Father, meaning God, such as, *Abida*—father of
knowledge; *Abidan*—father of judgment; *Abner*—father of
light; *Abigail*—father of joy; *Abihail*—father of might;

[9] *Divine Science, Its Principle and Practice.* Copyright 1957 By Divine
Science Church and College, Denver, Colorado.
[10] Pslams 89:26.
[11] I Chronicles 29:10.

*Abitub*—father of good; *Abishalom*—father of peace. "Name" in the Bible means nature. Here we have the Hebrews naming their children after the attributes of God. Jesus called God *Abba* which is the Aramaic word for *Ab* or father. *And he said, Abba, Father, all things are possible unto thee.*[12] Paul said, *Ye have received the Spirit of adoption, whereby we cry Abba, Father.*[13]

*Our Father* denotes the universal Father and establishes all men as brothers. For have we not a common father? The child is like the father, therefore, we inherit all that the Father is: life, light, power, truth, intelligence, wisdom, peace, joy, beauty. These three words alone constitute a complete treatment: recognition, realization, and release. If properly understood we could stop right here.

Our Father is omnipresent, omnipotent, and omniscient, which means everywhere present, all-powerful, and all-knowing. The child made in His image and likeness must then share these qualities. It is all wrapped up in the words, *Our Father.* Jesus told us in so many ways that he did not consider the Father his Father exclusively, but, *Our Father,* the Father of us all.

### Which Art in Heaven

The Pharisees demanded that Jesus tell them when the kingdom of God would come. He answered, *The kingdom of God cometh not with observation; Neither shall they say, Lo here!, or, lo there! for, behold, the kingdom of God*

---

12 Mark 14:36.                    13 Romans 8:15.

*is within you.*[14] Could he have made it any plainer? He located the kingdom of God, or the kingdom of heaven, right within us. J.B. Phillips in his translation put it this way: *The kingdom of God never comes by watching for it. Men cannot say, "Look, here it is," or "There it is," for the kingdom of God is inside you.*[15]

Heaven is not a place but a state of mind, the awareness of the Power and Presence of God with us. It is so clearly stated in the great prayer. We all share one Father, *Our Father,* one Source, one Creator, and the dominion of this awareness, the kingdom, is forever within us. Once we understand the hidden meaning in the Lord's Prayer it is impossible to think of ourselves as separated from the Perfect Power of God within us.

### Hallowed Be Thy Name

*Hallowed be thy name* means: wholeness is thy nature. The word hallowed is derived from the root word *halig* which means whole. Holy and holiness also come from *halig.* Holiness (wholeness) is one of the attributes of God that he bestows upon His image and likeness, man. If Thy nature is to be whole, our nature must be likewise. Wholeness is the complete trinity: spirit, mind, and body—all one. When Moses was told, *The place whereon thou standest is holy ground,*[16] it means, the wholeness of life is right where you are. We do not make anything out of anything, for Life already is complete, whole, and perfect.

14 Luke 17:20,21.
15 J. B. Phillips, *The Gospels* (New York: Macmillan Co., 1955).
16 Exodus 3:5.

When Moses understood that the *I Am* would tell him what to do and say, he was able to undertake the great task of leading the children of Israel out of Egypt. When we understand that the I Am, God within us, Emmanuel, is whole and perefct Life, all-knowing and intelligent, we are able to move from the known to the unknown with certainty and trust. Wherever we are, God is, there is the wholeness of Life.

## Thy Kingdom Come

*Thy kingdom come means* I am ready. Let Thy kingdom come in me. It is consent. It is agreement with Life. It is the acquiescence on our part that puts us in balance with God's perfect Life. Thy kingdom is already here. We need to receive it. It is now, not something that is to come at some future date. It is now and forever. The dominion of God is within you and everywhere present. Thy kingdom *is* come. Eternal means changeless. Thy kingdom is changeless perfection. This is the healing. How could anything be wrong?

## Thy Will Be Done in Earth As It Is in Heaven

Can we trust enough to say *Thy will be done?* What is the will of God? In the past we have thought of it as a disciplinary action to which we might grudgingly submit. But the will of God must coincide with the nature of God. We can trust the will of God when we understand that it must be in accord with the nature of God which is perfect, divine. The will of God is Love poured out in infinite measure for us.

In the past we have made God a scapegoat. When we didn't want to blame ourselves for the predicament we have gotten ourselves into, we blamed God. We said, "It was the will of God that I lost everything." Or, "I lost my child because it was the will of God." Or, "it is the will of God that I suffer and die." A man wrote me that he was in prison because it was the will of God. All this serves to dig ourselves deeper into the negative situation in a vain effort to avoid facing up to the Truth. *Thy will be done* might be said, "Let Thy perfect will be done." It is truly the highest form of prayer when rightly understood.

Glenn Clark used to remark, "I will to will the will of God."

When we let *Thy will be done* we have released the problem and the answer is there. As in heaven, so on earth; in other words, in spirit, mind, and body, I accept the Truth of my being. That which is in heaven (an awareness of God within) expresses Itself out into manifestation in our earthly experience. This indelibly impresses upon our minds that there is no separation between us and Our Father. The only separation has been in our own lack of understanding. As in Thy heaven, so in our earth, let Thy perfect will be done.

### Give Us This Day Our Daily Bread

Here we are not commanding God but accepting our daily bread, the bread of life, *that bread which cometh down from heaven, the living bread,* the spiritual Substance of all life which takes care of our every need. *I will rain bread from heaven for you.*[17]

As we trust in the divine Source of all good our every need will be provided. Just as the children of Israel received manna from heaven every day, so will we have our needs met. Manna, the bread that cometh down from heaven, is whatever is needed. It is the divine Substance that comes fresh each day for us.

### And Forgive Us Our Debts As We Forgive Our Debtors

Jesus told them, *For if ye forgive men their trespasses, your heavenly Father will also forgive you: But if ye forgive not men their trespasses, neither will your Father forgive your trespasses.*[18] He saw that this was the stumbling block to our prayers and so he gave them a few additional words on the subject at the conclusion of the Lord's Prayer.

There is only one sin (mistake), a sense of separation from God. Every sickness, every false deed, every accident, every evil thought stems from a feeling of being separated from our Source which is divine Love. Because he understood this, St. Augustine said, "Love and do what you please." When man has love in his heart it is impossible to sin.

Many people wonder why their prayers are not effective. Usually they are harboring some mental block that tends to separate them from an awareness of the Presence of God within them. Jesus pointed out on various occa-

17 Exodus 16:4.                18 Matthew 6:14, 15.

sions that it was necessary to forgive ourselves for past mistakes and to forgive others. In his prayer as related by Luke, he says, *And forgive us our sins; for we also forgive every one that is indebted to us.* He said that there was no difference whether he said *thy sins be forgiven thee, or, take up thy bed and walk.* When the stumbling block was removed the healing took place.

Resentment, hate, animosity, jealousy, or any other breed of negative thinking blocks the free flow of Spirit. God is Love, and when Love is given the opportunity, it will neutralize fear and all of the children of fear, such as anxiety, worry, jealousy, envy. However, one has to be ready and willing to release those negative feelings so that the free flow of the Spirit may bring about its perfect fulfillment in scientific prayer. God, as divine Love, can forgive us our sins, but we have to trust in divine Love instead of the destructive forces of fear and negation. When we think ill of another, we are trespassing upon the privacy of that person. When we think truth about another, we are helping to raise that person up in consciousness. That is what we do in prayer. We seek to be forgiven our gossip, our malicious thinking, our foolish thinking, and our negative feeling. When we forgive those who trespass against us we score a great victory of the spirit. The three ideas of recognition, realization, and release continually run through every segment of the Lord's Prayer. When we forgive another, we affirm the Truth of his being. We see the Presence of God where he is. When we forgive ourselves for past mistakes we recognize the Presence of God within us. Where we have been bound by a sense of separation from God we now are whole again, one with the

Father which is in heaven, able to receive his boundless good. Now our prayers can be answered, for we are willing to receive the answer.

## And Lead Us Not Into Temptation: But Deliver Us From Evil

This is one of the most difficult statements to understand. Try saying: "And God does not lead us into temptation but delivers us from evil." I have heard many say that they could not understand how God could lead us into temptation. This misunderstanding is due to a belief in God and man as separate entities. Let us go back for a moment to the three R's of prayer:

1. We recognize that God is everywhere present.
2. We realize that God is individualized in and through man.
3. We release ourselves to the Almighty Power.

The misunderstanding was due to the temptation to think of ourselves as being lowly and apart from God, a God apart from us. The evil we ask to be delivered from is the error of false thinking, the belief that there is power in the false appearances of life.

God does not lead us into temptation. It is we who let ourselves be tempted by the appearances.

I talked to a man who had lost fifty thousand dollars in the stock market. A stock he owned had dropped ten points in two days. He was so morose that he could not be lifted by any words of encouragement. You see, he was placing his faith in the price of the stock and not in the ability of God to supply his needs at all times.

How would you feel if the business for which you had labored for twenty-five years had to go into bankruptcy? Would you be tempted to lose your trust in God?

How would you feel if your livelihood depended upon your ability to sing professionally, and suddenly and without any explanation you lost your voice. Would you be tempted to worry?

Suppose you were discharged from your job and circumstances prevented you from getting another, causing you to have to live on a small reserve. Would you be tempted to be anxious about the future?

Suppose you had been married for ten years, you had three young children, and your husband was killed, leaving you no insurance. Would you be tempted to deny God and condemn your fate?

Do you see what is meant by the statement renouncing temptation? We cannot let anything cause us to be tempted to deny the Presence of God as our supply, as our life, as the very substance of our being. When everything was taken away from Job, his wealth, his prestige, and even his family, his wife urged him to curse God and die. She was trying to lead him into temptation. But Job refused to do this. We, too, must affirm with Job in the face of adversity, *Though he slay me, yet will I trust in him.*[19] All that we need is still right where we are. Through faith are we delivered from evil.

This, then, is the request, that we be given the insight and the understanding that we may be delivered out of

[19] Job 13:15.

erroneous thinking into a realization that the Power lives through us in perfect ways.

*For Thine Is The Kingdom and The Power and The Glory Forever.*

The human inclination is to sing praise to God when things go right, to doubt His very existence when things, according to our judgment, seem to go wrong. There is an old saying, "Forever is a long, long time." Can you acknowledge that *Thine is the kingdom and the power and the glory* day in and day out forever? This is praying without ceasing. It is a powerful affirmation that will overcome any difficulty. It is an affirming of the wonder and the glory and the Power and the Wisdom and the Truth of God right where you are. It is the summing up of all of your faith and of the flawless Truth revealed in the prayer of Jesus.

*Amen*

Have you ever wondered why we say *Amen* at the end of a prayer or sing it at the end of a hymn? *Amen* as an adjective in the New Testament signifies *firm* and *faithful.* In Isaiah 65:16 the God of amen (Hebrew) is translated *God of Truth.* In its adverbial sense, amen means *certainly, truly, surely.* The amen of Jesus is translated *verily* and we often have a double verily—*verily, verily I say unto you*—which in the Hebrew would be *amen and amen.* We would say, "Truly, truly, I say to you." The double form is for emphasis. *Amen* used at the end of the prayer means

*So be it,* or, *So it is,* or, *It is so.* Some say, *So let it be.*
Amen!

## THE PERFECT PRAYER

Our Father, Feeder, Provider, Protector, First Cause, Divine
Principle, Creator, and Sustainer of all Good. Thou art everywhere present, all-knowing, all-powerful; Love made manifest
as Thy own perfect creation. Wholeness is Thy nature, and
we, Thy image and likeness, are forever whole as we portray
Thee.

In Thy kingdom there is no sickness, sin, or lack. Thy
kingdom is Love expressing as harmonious right action in
every phase of Life. Thy kingdom is established; as in Thy
heaven within, so it is in our earth.

Feed us with Thy word, the bread of Life.

We know that our sins are forgiven us to the degree that we
are able to forgive. Let Thy Love flow through us to all mankind.

In overcoming temptation, we are delivered from evil. There
is no power apart from Thee.

Thine is the kingdom and we, through Love and Law, are
given dominion over all the world; but the Power and the
Glory, from first to last, belong to Thee. Amen. And so it is.

# SIX

---

## What the Miracles of Jesus
## Teach Us Today

*Then gathered the chief priests and the Pharisees a council,
and said, What do we? for this man doeth many miracles.*
                                                        —John 11:47

There are many facets to the teaching of the Master.
Through the healing miracles he attracted not only the
multitudes but many of his disciples. It was the miracles
that held their attention and provided him with a listening
audience and through the miracles he taught the Truth in
a most revealing way.

They followed him for the loaves and fishes and the
spectacular phenomena, and after he started giving them
the mystical teaching as found in the book of John his
followers fell away. Like people today they were concerned with things in the outer world and were not ready
for the esoteric (inner) teaching.

How fortunate we are today that the miracles were recorded for us, for they contain the mystical teaching, the
awareness of the Oneness of the Spirit of God with the
spirit of man. As with the parables he used in his teaching

ministry, the healing miracles each contain expressions of one or more great lessons in Truth. Let us see what some of these great Truths are.

## He Taught Us Not to Judge by Appearances But to Judge Righteous Judgment

He told them: *Judge not according to the appearance, but judge righteous judgment.*[1] The healing miracles of Jesus, without exception, were based on his ability to see through the appearances to the Truth of Being and so he gave us this commandment out of his own experience in healing. He did not mean that we were to be like the ostrich and bury our heads in the sand, but that we were, even while seeing the appearance, to look beyond it to the reality of Life.

As Jesus walked through a crowd he knew the Truth about the people around him. At no time was he caught up in the appearance of suffering that confronted him. Hence, the woman with an issue of blood was instantly healed as she touched him.

When the man stood before him with a withered arm, he did not see a withered arm. He saw a man who was whole, complete, and perfect. And so he said, *Stretch forth thine hand.*[2] There was never any doubt but that the man would be able to stretch it forth.

When Lazarus was in his tomb, Jesus ordered the stone to be taken away. Martha objected on the grounds that her brother was dead and that by this time his body would

[1] John 7:24.                    [2] Matthew 12:13.

stink. He had been dead four days. But Jesus did not accept this. He had told her that if she would believe, she would see the glory of God. The stone was taken away and Jesus lifted up his eyes (took his attention away from the appearance of death and looked to the high Consciousness of Life) and said, *Father, I thank thee that thou hast heard me . . . but because of the people which stand by I said it, that they may believe that thou hast sent me.* And then he said in a loud voice, *Lazarus, come forth.* Then Lazarus appeared, even though he was bound hand and foot he appeared.[3]

Jesus did not see death, he saw Life, Life indestructible. This Life is perfect.

Jesus did not see a lack of wine at the wedding feast . . . he saw an abundance of good wine there. No, Jesus did not hypnotize anyone into believing that the water was wine. He had the faith, the courage, and the understanding to know that that which appeared to be water was wine and there was no part of life that could resist his knowing.

Remember when he entered the house of Simon Peter and found his mother-in-law was ill of a great fever. You and I might say in such a situation, "Look, this doesn't seem like a good time for you to have guests for dinner. I'll take a rain check and come back another time." But Jesus was not caught up in the appearances. *He stood over her and rebuked the fever; and it left her: and immediately she arose and ministered unto them.*[4] Rebuking the fever was denying it. As we would say to the symptoms of a cold, "You have no power over me. Get out of me right

---

[3] John 11:41-44.                    [4] Luke 4:39.

now." So clearly did he look through the appearances to the Truth of Being that she got up at once and apparently forgot all about the fever. Certainly she took no time out to convalesce.

## He Taught That It Is Done Unto You As You Believe

He said unto the centurion, *As thou hast believed so be it done unto thee.* And to the blind man he asked the question, *Believe ye that I am able to do this?* And he said, after withering the fig tree, *And all things, whatsoever ye shall ask in prayer, believing, ye shall receive.*[5]

Another time when Jesus was walking along and they brought to him the boy who had fits, the one whom the disciples were unable to heal, he said to the boy's father, *If thou canst believe, all things are possible to him that believeth.* The father understood this and cried out, *Lord, I believe; help thou mine unbelief.*[6] And when the disciples took Jesus aside and asked him why they were unable to heal the boy, he told them, *Because of your unbelief.* And he then took the opportunity of giving them a lesson on faith: *For verily I say unto you, if ye have faith as a grain of mustard seed, ye shall say unto this mountain, Remove hence to yonder place, and it shall remove and nothing shall be impossible unto you.*[7]

[5] Matthew 8:13; 9:28; 21:22.      [6] Mark 9:23, 24.
[7] Matthew 17:20.

## *The Healings of Jesus Were Instantaneous*

Everything that he taught was in the present tense. Every healing was instantaneous. He did not say to the man with a withered arm, "You poor man, I feel sorry for you. I'll pray that you will get better as time goes on." No. He said, *stretch forth thine hand. Now* was clearly implied.

He taught that *the kingdom of heaven is at hand.* At hand *now. I am the way, the truth and the life*—not I will be.

In every case of healing, he accepted the perfection of God in Mind and that which he accepted became manifest. *And immediately his leprosy was cleansed—And immediately their eyes received sight—And immediately the fever left her—And immediately he arose, took up the bed, and went forth before them all—And straightway the damsel arose and walked—And immediately he received his sight— And immediately the man was made whole*—and on and on. Did you doubt that it could happen immediately?

The time lag with most of us is the time that it takes to build the faith that Jesus never was without.

## *His Teaching Was Absolute Obedience to The Word of Christ*

How often today, having received our instructions from the voice within, we fail to heed those instructions. We pray for answers and when those answers come we are often too stubborn to follow them through to victory.

*And they were astonished at his doctrine: for his word*

*was with power.*[8] In nearly every healing recorded in the Gospels there is a command made that must be obeyed. Jesus expected the person seeking help to act as though he were healed. *Tabitha arise.*[9] She did. And when the dead man was carried out from the city to him, he touched his bier and said to him: *Young man I say unto thee, arise. And he that was dead sat up, and began to speak.*[10] Jesus declared the Truth about those who came to him for healing and they believed him and acted upon it.

But do we always do the same? How often we say, "God is my health," only to wonder again how long the sickness will last!

A woman in her eighties was told by the doctors that she had terminal cancer. And so it did appear to those around her, for she had wasted away to the extent that it seemed that she was about to pass on. She was unable to take any nourishment and her family daily awaited the news of her death.

However, the patient herself had not given up. She continued to seek a healing. She worked with a spiritual practitioner and together they continued to affirm the Truth of her Being, knowing that she was a divine idea in the Mind of God; that God saw her whole and perfect, made in His image and likeness. They denied the power of the disease, and knew that there was no power in the word, "cancer." At what you might call "the eleventh hour" there was a dramatic change in her condition. The woman was healed. Again she was able to enjoy life without any

8 Luke 4:32.                                        9 Mark 5:41.
10 Luke 7:14, 15.

of the former symptoms. Her healing was so apparent to all who knew her that even the skeptics accepted it as a fact. The doctors were amazed and could not explain the change in her condition.

*He Proved the Power of the Word and by Example Showed That One Did Not Have to Be Present to Speak the Healing Word Effectively*

The story of Jesus healing the servant of the centurian illustrates the power of the spoken word, the word that is spoken with authority. It proves that it is possible to take dominion over the world. It further points up the fact that it is not necessary for the one speaking his word to be present where the sick person is, for here we have a good example of what we would call absent treatment. Moreover, it was a clear example of instantaneous healing as well as of two agreeing in faith. *If two of you shall agree on earth as touching any thing they shall ask, it shall be done for them of my Father which is in heaven.*[11]

Again and again he spoke his word with absolute authority: *Be thou clean; Receive thy sight; Arise, take up thy bed and walk.* And could anything be more dramatic than the withering of the fig tree? Could anything be clearer? It reminds me of one time when I was the minister of a large, city church. We had been talking in the Sunday School classes about the book, *The Power of Prayer on Plants* by Dr. Franklin Loehr.[12] The children

11 Matthew 18:19.
12 Franklin Loehr, *The Power of Prayer on Plants* (New York: New American Library, 1969).

made actual experiments following the diagrams in the book. Identical circumstances were set up for two pans of plants. The same amount of water was given each pan. It was truly a scientifically controlled situation. The children blessed one pan each day, praying for them and recognizing the power of God at work in them. The plants in the other pan were condemned and told that they could not grow. In other words, like the fig tree, they were *cursed*. When the children brought in the various pans in which the seeds had been planted and watered, it was found that there was a definite difference between the pans blessed and those that had been condemned. Pictures were taken and charts made showing that the pans that had been blessed grew seedlings twice as tall as the pans that had been condemned. In fact, the pans that had not received the blessing of affirmative prayer but had been condemned to die actually did have plants that shriveled and died. It was a vivid example of the power of the spoken word.

*He Demonstrated That Giving Thanks Before the Answer Comes Reenforces Our Mental Acceptance of the Healing*

"Thanking you in advance for your kind favors" is an old-fashioned phrase that used to be used in business letters. Usually these letters were signed, "Your obedient servant." Jesus approached the Father in this trusting manner. He expected the Grace of God to act in his behalf and he was an obedient servant who went about doing the will of Him that sent him. Therefore, he did not doubt that his prayers would be answered. He kept the first commandment and this was the covenant.

Picture Jesus standing in front of the tomb of Lazarus. He did not waste any time thinking of Lazarus in his grave clothes, the body already disintegrating. Instead, he gave thanks that his prayer had been heard even before he spoke his word. He did so to point out his approach that they might understand.

When the multitude needed to be fed he commanded over four thousand to sit down on the ground. Considering this was like a picnic it was like saying, "Come to the table." And he took the few loaves and fishes *and gave thanks,* and then he fed them all and when they had finished there were seven baskets full left over!

When your healing seems slow in coming, try giving thanks first and see how it replenishes your faith!

*Ye Shall Know the Truth and the Truth Shall Make You Free*

What did Jesus mean by *ye shall know the truth and the truth shall make you free?* In the first place, it was said to *those Jews which believed on him* and he also said *If ye continue in my word, then are ye my disciples indeed.*[13] These were his disciples, the men he had taught day after day, and he told them that they were to continue following his teaching if they would know the truth that would set them free. Every healing was a matter of knowing the Truth that set somebody free.

Julian of Norwich said, "I cannot see sin for God."

13 John 8:31, 32.

Jesus put it that the pure in heart see God. The pure in heart, those who steadfastly follow the commandments of the Christ, see only God and therefore they are free from the natural law of sin, sickness, and death. He understood this so clearly and wanted all mankind to share his awareness.

## Forgiveness and Healing Are Synonymous

He used one famous healing miracle as an opportunity to point out that there was no difference in forgiving a man's sins or telling him to take up his bed and walk. To the man sick of the palsy who had been lowered through the ceiling he said, *Son, be of good cheer; thy sins be forgiven thee.* He intuitively perceived that certain of the scribes were critical of him in their hearts. The scribes considered that only God had the power to forgive sins. So Jesus pointed out, *Wherefore think ye evil in your hearts? For whether is easier to say, Thy sins be forgiven thee; or to say, Arise and walk? But that ye may know that the Son of man hath power on earth to forgive sins, (then sayeth he to the sick of the palsy) Arise, take up thy bed, and go unto thine house. And he arose and departed to his house.*[14]

When we ask that we may know the Truth we must be prepared to part with our erroneous thinking. Every healing has its price. Usually there is some area of darkness in our consciousness that needs the light of Truth to shine upon it. If we have been slow in receiving a healing it is well to ask, "What is the particular area of my thinking

[14] Matthew 9:2-7.

that needs clarification? Is there someone I need to forgive? Do I need to forgive myself? Do I need to forgive God if I am blaming God for the predicament in which I find myself?" Forgiveness plays such an important part in getting rid of neurotic thought patterns.

In *You Can Heal Yourself* Dr. Masaharu Taniguchi, spiritual leader of millions in Japan, gives case after case of cancer that was healed once the patient was willing to part with some past grudge, to forgive the self or others.

A person would do well to take an inventory of his thinking and see where he can remove old stumbling blocks that are hindering his spiritual growth and preventing him from receiving a healing. This is what Jesus meant when he said, *Repent ye, the kingdom of Heaven is at hand.* Repent means to turn around, to change one's thinking. So we could paraphrase the quotation: Change your thinking about yourself and others, the dominion of perfect right action is at hand.

## Jesus Used No Set Formula for His Miracles

Most people like the security of having a formula for everything. To get a particular result, it should be done this way, they say. Jesus did not use any particular formula for the purpose of establishing a belief within the mind of the person for whom the miracle was performed. One time he mixed clay and spittle to put on the eyes of a blind man; many times he laid his hands on the person; then again he stuck his fingers in the ears of a deaf man; at other times he just spoke his word, commanding the person to rise or some demon (symptom) to be removed.

Although he recited a prayer when he was asked to teach his disciples to pray, he usually never mentioned prayer as he went about his healing work. You will note that Jesus did much praying alone. He built up his consciousness by going apart and communing with the Father. By living in the Presence he was living in a continual state of prayer. People were healed by just being in his presence or by touching his clothing. I like to think of Jesus as one who was always "prayed up." He embodied the consciousness of healing at all times, so that he was ready when the need arose.

He used any means necessary to build the faith that would bring about the healing.

He told the lepers who had been healed to go and tell no man. He did this because he realized that the doubts of others could impinge upon the faith of the one healed.

What does this mean to us today? Many people are superstitious about spiritual things. They believe that putting one's trust in God precludes any human steps such as good nutrition or exercise. I think that Jesus, by example, clearly indicated that we are to ask for guidance and then take such human footsteps as our inner guidance indicates. Man is a triune being: spirit, mind, and body. We are living in a physical world and although the healing is spiritual it manifests itself in the physical body. A spiritual healing translates itself into right thinking and right thinking manifests as right living. Remember, the glory belongs to God, the only Power and the only Life.

## *And This Is Not All*

We have mentioned just a few of the miracles that came through Jesus. I believe the Bible mentions thirty-seven in the Gospels, but there were many more.

The important thing I want to leave with you is that the Christ, the Son of God in you, is still the Way. The Power that Jesus used is still active and to It nothing is impossible.

All we have to remember is to follow the teaching of Jesus who understood healing and practiced it so successfully. We have tried to highlight some of the facets, some of the Truths that he taught here, but other ideas will come to you as you read again and again the healing miracles of Jesus. You will see things that are important to you, things that you need to see right at that moment and the teaching will live again for you as if it had been written down just for that very moment. Remember that there is one Power, the Power of God, and it is available to you at all times . . . . . . . . . . . *for thine is the Kingdom and the Power and the Glory for ever. Amen.*

### GOD IS THE ONLY POWER IN MY LIFE

God is the only power in my life. Nothing from without can touch the perfect Life of God within. No past experience has power over me. I am a perfect child of God and nothing that anyone has ever done or said can interfere with my divine inheritance. The power of God is greater than any circumstance in my life. The strength of God is mine to use.

Turning away from all feelings of inadequacy, I discover that all that I need is within me now. As I forgive the past I find that I have nothing to atone for, nothing to run away from. Casting off the old self, I discover my true Self. I take dominion in my life. Old habits have no power over me. Conditions have no power over me. Personalities have no power over me. I take dominion. I am whole—I am free—I am complete *now and forever more.*

And so it is.

# SEVEN

## When Is a Miracle?

*Miracle, N. (from the Latin miraculum, mirari—to wonder.)*
*An event or effect in the physical world deviating from the*
*known laws of nature, or transcending our knowledge of these*
*laws.—Webster's Collegiate Dictionary*

*And they went forth, and preached everywhere, the Lord*
*working with them, and confirming the word with signs fol-*
*lowing.—Mark 16:20*

And so it continues down to this day. Whenever man's
faith has admitted the Power there have been *signs fol-*
*lowing* which man called miracles. The word "miracle"
is a relative word. As *Webster's* states, a miracle is an event
that transcends *our knowledge* of the law. Since we live in
a universe of law and order, some have questioned whether
we should call these wondrous events miracles.

In this chapter we shall consider a number of rather
spectacular healings and I will leave it up to you whether
they should be called miracles.

John Locke wrote: "A miracle I take to be a sensible
operation, which being above the comprehension of the
spectator, and in his opinion contrary to the established
courses of nature, is taken by him to be divine."

The miracle I am about to describe to you was undoubtedly a law-abiding event to the Almighty, but to those of us who witnessed it, it seemed pretty much like a miracle.

I want you to know I take no personal credit for this event. True, I did the prayer work, but there is more to the phenomenon that the world calls a miracle than that. As we said in chapter three, the spiritual mind practitioner offers the patient his faith in the Almighty Power of God. If the patient is willing to be healed, the Power goes to work and the healing takes place. The common denominator of all healing is still to be found in the statement made by the Master, *it is done unto you as you believe.* Jack Addington never healed anybody of himself. As our friend, Paul, said, *There is no power but of God.*[1] It is very important that we understand this Truth because without it there is no healing. All through the Bible we find it brought out by those who received the Truth: *Power belongeth unto God.*[2]

Back in 1958, at the suggestion of a mutual friend, a handsome young man came to see me. Walter ("Buzz") Forward was the president of an insurance company. My first impression was, "Here's a young fellow who has everything it takes to be happy—youth, a pleasing personality, and early success." I soon discovered that he was far from happy. You see, Buzz had lost 70 percent of his hearing. He couldn't even hear the telephone ring. He couldn't enjoy television, radio, or go to a movie. It made him extremely nervous to be in groups of people. He told me that he had been to the best medical specialists available

[1] Romans 13:1.  [2] Psalms 62:11.

and none of them had been able to do anything for him.

"I've come to you," he said, "because our mutual friend, Jim Bourland, suggested I should talk to you. He told me that your first wife had had a very unusual healing that had the doctors baffled. I'll be frank with you," he went on. "When Jim asked me if I believed in spiritual healing, I told him 'Nope, I don't believe in all that nonsense.' "

But, there he was, sitting across from me at my desk and I was talking to him, talking to him about the spiritual laws of life, the laws I am talking to you about in this book. I talked to him about spiritual mind healing, and, although he said he couldn't hear a word I said, (I wrote notes to him) he sat still while I had a treatment out loud for him. I continued to give him absent treatment every day. For three weeks he came for counseling and we proceeded along the same lines, mostly communicating in the Silence.

I discovered as we proceeded that the physical problem, the deafness, wasn't the only thing that was bothering him. He was very nervous, probably as a result of the deafness, and, as usual, the body was the outer picture of an inner sickness. Things were out of balance in this young man's life. He was not happy in his home life, his work did not please him; in short, he was not in tune with Life (with a capital L). Since we are using his name (with his permission) we won't go into all of the details. The point is that a healing of the whole man was needed.

My treatment was that Buzz was one with the wholeness of Life. I kept affirming that Life in all its perfection flowed through him and through every part of his experience. I asked, in the Silence, that he hear only the voice of God. By that I meant that he hear with the inner ear the Truth that would set him free; that he know himself as the image and likeness of God, perfect as his Creator, the wondrous Life within him. I kept recognizing the Power within him, refusing to be influenced by the fact that he thought the whole business was a lot of malarkey. At the third session I suggested he attend my church the next Sunday.

"I tried that once," he said. "My mother talked me into it. I got so nervous, sitting there and not being able to hear that I was wringing wet at the end of the service. I don't want to go through that again!"

I told him to come anyway, that I had something to say that would interest him. He shook his head doubtfully as he left.

But Buzz did come to church that Sunday. He came and heard every word that I said. He was beaming when he shook my hand afterward in the line. I never saw a person happier.

Today I talked to him, fifteen years later, and he told me that he has heard perfectly ever since that day.

Of even more importance to me, he has found himself. He is in balance with Life, and he is very happy in every area of his life. He has remarried and I could tell right away that this was a most successful union. He loves his work. He is now the president of the Wilshire Forward Company, a large printing business in Los Angeles. "I always wanted to be a cowboy," he told me, "now I'm a weekend cowboy with a two-acre ranch and four horses. I've got everything going for me," was the way he put it. "Some would call it a miracle," he said. "Knowing what

I know, what you taught me about Life, it would have been a miracle if it hadn't happened!"

He has "everything going for him," indeed. All of Life is with him. It was never against him. It was with him fifteen years ago even when he did not know it.

How do I explain the change in his health and affairs? Somewhere along the line he let Life flow through him in its perfect way. Everyone wants to express divine Wholeness. Deep within, each one longs to go back to what Jesus called *The glory which I had with thee before the world was.* The perfect Life within is there. It is the Healer. It knows only Wholeness. When we align ourselves with this Wholeness the "miracle" takes place. The body is a sort of barometer that indicates the health of the soul. The physical healing is just what you might call a by-product of the real healing, the healing of the whole man. As Buzz put it: "It would have been a miracle if it hadn't happened!"

*Except Ye Become As Little Children*

Children seem to respond very quickly to prayer. Perhaps it is because they have not built up a resistance to the wonder and glory of Life through what their elders consider logic.

A friend of ours dropped by one afternoon and we got to talking about miraculous healings we had known firsthand. This led her to write to me the next day to share this one with us.

When my daughter, Meredith, was about three, a tragic thing happened in our home. Our house has a slow-moving elevator to the downstairs. It has a safety contraption that will not permit the door to open when the elevator is in motion. Somehow our three year old had her tiny hand against the back door jamb when her sister, Alison, slammed the door shut and started the elevator. Her father and I were downstairs but we could tell by her screams that something dreadful had happened. He ran outside and up while I had to stay downstairs until that slow-moving elevator got down. One of the most wonderful things about treatment (scientific prayer) is that it gives you something constructive to do in a panic situation. I spent those long minutes treating until I could go up to her. When I finally got there, Leonard had released the door and her hand was cut wide open clear across the palm. For some reason we could not reach the doctor. As her father washed the little hand in cold water to ease the pain, I continued treating. This happened about five o'clock in the afternoon. By bedtime the hand had never bled and by morning there was no sign where the cut had been, nor did it ever show a bruise. We all considered this a miracle.

This story brings to my mind something that happened in my wife's family. Again, since she was there and witnessed it, I will let her tell it in her own words:

One evening my mother and I and my two brothers and two sisters were packing the remains of a picnic lunch, having spent the day at the lake. Because of the lateness of the hour we were all hurrying to stow things away in the car and get on the road before it got dark. Somehow in the confusion, somebody slammed the door of our big old-fashioned Buick, a very heavy door, saying, "Everybody in?" And then, we realized that little Roger's hand had been shut in the hinge of the door. I think he was about six years old at the time.

Because we had been brought up believing in the power of prayer, "knowing the Truth," as we called it, there were no cries of "Oh, how terrible, let me see it!" No one spoke during the long journey home. We were all busy, each in his own way treating (using scientific prayer) for Roger. Toward the end of the trip—I suppose it took about an hour those days to drive home from the lakeshore, our spirits were lifted. We all believed that his little hand was healed even though we had heard the door slam and had helped him take his hand out of the hinge. Even now I marvel at our faith, the faith of little children and a mother who believed in miracles. When we looked at Roger's hand in the bright light of the kitchen, there was no bruise, no broken bones, not even a scratch. Down through the years we have all remembered this event. We considered it a miracle.

## The Woman Who Overcame Her Little Hates

I have this woman's story in her own words on a tape recording. She gave me full permission to use the story and to use her name. Millie Whitmarsh was suffering from a condition diagnosed by doctors as cancer of the lymph glands. The disease had progressed to where she had an open, running sore under each ear. She had been told that there was no hope for her recovery. In other words, she had been given the ultimatum that strikes terror to the minds of many people, *terminal cancer.* But Millie didn't accept the verdict. She refused to accept the diagnosis as final. She decided to go away by herself and pray and meditate until she was healed. *She believed that she could be healed, and this is very important.*

Now, this is the interesting part. She realized that she had some problems in her own thinking that needed clarification before she could be healed. There was something she had to give up in order to be healed. One thing Millie told me was that she had always feared being alone. She could not spend a single night alone. If her husband was going to be out of town, she would have to have someone stay with her. Also, she hated doing housework. She had, she told me, a series of what she called "little hates," and it came to her that she should get rid of these little hates.

Didn't Jesus say: *Ye shall know the truth and the truth shall make you free?* This was the Truth that set Millie free. She saw that she needed to get rid of her little hates and she was willing to do something about it. First, she did something that was, for her, a real right about face. She went out to the desert and stayed all alone in a travel trailer. Now just imagine a person who *hated* staying alone at night, all alone in a trailer miles from anyone. At night, the coyotes howled and the wind whistled around the trailer. There were not even any other trailers nearby. She was completely alone. When she was frightened she literally talked out loud to God. She filled her days with prayer and meditation.

Something wonderful happened. She said she began to lose her little hates. All of a sudden she didn't hate to be alone anymore. She had also hated doing dishes and now she didn't mind doing the dishes either. All of the old patterns of resistance had left her. She felt companioned by the Spirit. Day after day, she walked and talked with God. It was a beautiful time in her life, one that she would always remember.

And then, the miracle happened. Each one must receive his healing in his own way, at his own point of awareness. Millie had a vision. Now, I don't mean to imply for a moment that it is necessary to have a vision to have a healing. I am only telling you what happened to Millie. She said that she felt that Jesus stood behind her. She couldn't see him, but she could feel his presence behind her and she felt that he put his hands over her ears. *In that moment she was healed!* She knew it. When she went to look in the mirror the ugly running sores had disappeared. They had been draining constantly but now there was not even any moisture on her skin *and there were no scars left to show that there had been holes at one time beneath each ear.* She asked me to examine her neck and I did so. Her skin was as smooth as a child's. It was hard to believe that it had ever been otherwise. There was no doubt in her mind that she had experienced an instantaneous healing. She glowed as she told me about it. Her family considered it a miracle. What do you think?

After that, I began to watch for mental blocks that might be keeping other people from receiving a healing and I found that there was some truth to this. Often there were deep-rooted guilts or resentments directed at some other person that blocked the door to a realization of the Presence of God in the person's life. Sometimes these people were not willing, as Millie was, to trade their hates and fears for the healing, but when they were, the healing took place. I mention this because there may be those who read this chapter who have been wondering why their prayers were not answered.

If you are wondering why your healing seemed to be denied you, ask yourself: "Are there some little hates I need to leave behind? Where do I need to let the light shine in the darkness of my own mind? What can I give up that I may be receptive to my healing?" Pray: That I may know the truth. Ask it over and over: That I may know the truth, and then be willing to accept the Truth and act upon it when it is revealed to you. I firmly believe *there are no incurable diseases.* If Millie could be healed of cancer of the lymph glands which she had been told was incurable, then anyone can be healed if he is willing to receive that healing.

## Healing Left Her Healthier Than Ever Before

I visited a young woman in a hospital at the request of her mother. The mother told me that the doctors had diagnosed the case as terminal cancer; that her daughter was now in the last stages of the disease, and they did not expect to take her home from the hospital. If one were to judge by appearances, this was true. There was a gray pallor to her skin and she had lost so much weight that her arms were skin and bones. I asked her if she believed that she could be healed and her answer was "Yes." We had a spiritual mind treatment together.

A year later I saw the mother and her opening remark was, "Have you heard? My daughter whom you visited at Grossmont Hospital is going to have another baby. She had an instantaneous healing following your visit at the hospital and has never felt better in her life." Putting the pieces together, I found that the daughter had started to get well immediately after our treatment together and within the week had walked out of the hospital.

*Man's Extremity Is God's Opportunity*

In my work I hear of many miracles. My files are full of stories of amazing healings in which a whole sequence of cause and effect has suddenly changed through a turning to the divine Presence. Recently I received a letter telling me of just such a thrilling incident.

Some months ago I published in an issue of *Abundant Living,* the magazine that goes out every month to my students, a little poem which has been known and loved by my family for years.

> I am the light that God shines through,
> For He and I are one, not two.
> He wants me where and as I am,
> I need not fear, nor will, nor plan.
> But, if I am relaxed and free,
> Then He'll work out His plan through me.

My sister-in-law, who lives in Shreveport, Louisiana, wrote me that she used this little verse as a devotional for the Episcopal Woman's Guild to which she belongs and it was enthusiastically received. Many asked her for copies. I am quoting from her letter:

A young woman called last night to say: "I thought you would like to know of an experience I had last week. I had a late dentist appointment for a severe and lengthy disorder. Before going to have this done I took my oldest son to a birthday party from which he was to return with a friend and left the two other children with a neighbor. [Her husband is gone much of the time as he is in the service.] At the party the children played football and my son was critically injured. By the time they located me it was getting dark and they urged me to come to the emergency room at the hospital immediately. I am afraid to drive at night and was in a panic state.

"As I tried to put the key in the ignition I shook so that it seemed impossible to make the drive. Suddenly your face was in front of me and your voice stated, 'I am the light.' I had made no effort to learn the prayer but it had made a deep impression on me when you gave it at the Guild meeting. At the time it did not seem strange that I knew it word for word, from beginning to end. In calm and confidence, I kept repeating it. Every light turned green as I approached it. I knew that all was well with my son and that we were in God's care.

"When I arrived at the hospital, twenty minutes later, I walked into the emergency room where seven doctors stood around the examining table. The decision to remove the spleen had just been canceled and for the first time, ten minutes before, my son had come out of shock and his vital signs were normal. Two doctors, one who had seen such cases for over twenty years, said that this was the first case which had not required operation in their experience. Many had been fatal.

"I am calling to thank you. Now I will learn the prayer. For the life of me I could not recite it to you even now!"

This from a woman who knew nothing of Spiritual Mind Healing and had never even attended our Episcopal healing service on Tuesday mornings.

I suppose that it won't seem unusual to you, but thought you would like to know of it.

I am always glad to have reports like these to share with others.

What happened here? Why did the course of natural events change so dramatically? Is it possible to explain a miracle?

## Are There Miracles?

Most people live by the law of cause and effect, which religions of the East call karma. A miracle is the manifestation of divine Law. When we live by the law of cause and effect, we are living according to our past mistakes, our old mistaken thinking. In this universe of law and order, we reap the thoughts we have sown. For every effect there is a cause.

But, when we go to First Cause—*Thou Great First Cause, least understood* [3]—when we live by Divine Law, the effect is still like the Cause but working from the supernatural makes it a miracle.

A miracle has to be a law-abiding event. Every miracle is in accord with Divine Law. God and His creation are One. God, the only Cause and Creator, the Essence of all Life, could only create out of Itself. That is why Jesus could say, *Be ye perfect even as your Father in heaven is perfect.* You see, the interesting thing is that once a miracle is understood, it ceases to be a miracle. We experience what we believe!

## The Time for Miracles Is Now

Did you think that all the miracles took place at the time of Jesus? Have you ever known anyone who experienced a dramatic physical healing? If you were to ask me that question, so many would come to mind that I could not possibly tell you all of them.

You know, it is very interesting—when we start think-

[3] Alexander Pope, *The Universal Prayer.*

ing about miracles, accepting miracles, expecting miracles, we find that we experience miracles. A miracle is a law-abiding event that may be a little bit over our heads but is thoroughly understood in Divine Mind.

I would like to share with you two dramatic healings that it was my privilege to witness. Both were healings of brain tumor, and although one of the patients was a ten-year-old girl and the other a man of retirement age, they had something else in common. In each case, when the person had come to me, I had been led to ask, "Do you believe that you can be healed?" In each case the answer had been, "Yes."

In the first instance, a family came to see me as a last resort, a father and mother and their five children, a handsome family, devoted to each other. They were all especially devoted to the little sister about whom they had come to see me. It seemed that the little girl had for some time been experiencing violent headaches. There was a great pressure in her head and recently her eyes had started to cross so that she could no longer focus them properly. They had taken this pretty little girl from one specialist to another. Endless tests had been made, even to boring a little hole in her head which, they said, was the way that the doctors go about diagnosing a brain tumor. And now the little girl was scheduled to be operated on the following Thursday. They were all so anxious about her, so eager to help the little sister. Their anxious glances kept returning to her again and again.

"Do you think that God can heal your sister?" I asked them. The answer was a quick "Yes."

This was a Catholic family and I have found that people

of this faith have a strong belief in God which causes them to respond very well to spiritual mind treatment.

Well, to make a long story short, we had a good treatment together. It was a powerful prayer, a complete surrender of the situation. After we had given thanks together for the healing, their faces brightened. You could see that they all felt better, that they had really accepted the miracle. And there was a miracle. Something happened that the doctors just couldn't understand.

To begin with, the little girl's headache was gone the next day. Her eyes were no longer crossed. In fact, she felt so well that she begged to go to the beach. The mother was so happy to have her interested again in having a good time that she gave her permission without any discussion. The family had a most enjoyable weekend together and the following Monday I heard from the mother.

She was worried, not about the little daughter who was feeling wonderful, she was worried as to what she should do about the doctor, about the arrangements that had been made with the hospital for the operation. Should they continue preparation for the operation scheduled for the following Thursday?

I countered with another question, "Do you think that she needs an operation?"

"No," replied the mother, "there doesn't seem to be anything wrong with her."

"Why don't you call your doctor and explain this to him," I suggested.

She did as I suggested and the doctor advised postponing the operation for a week. At the end of that time they would see what was indicated. At the end of the second week there was still no recurrence of the headaches or of the crossing of the eyes. There was never any further need of an operation. It is healings like this that convince us that there are no incurable diseases. To God nothing is impossible.

The man, whom I mentioned, had a similar experience. He, too, had been experiencing violent headaches which led him to have extensive tests resulting in a diagnosis of brain tumor. In his case, the symptoms had been slightly different. While he did not have the crossing of the eyes, he did experience a sense of imbalance. He said that he felt like he was walking on the side of a hill. Every now and then he reeled as if he was under the influence of liquor. This, he told me, was considered to be a pretty reliable symptom of brain tumor. The medical tests confirmed it. He, too, was scheduled for an operation when he came to see me.

Again, something told me to ask him, "Do you believe that God can heal you?" He answered, "Yes," without a moment's hesitation. I will always believe that the healing took place in that moment of agreement.

We joined together in a treatment.

"I feel better already," he said as he left my office.

Several weeks later I called him to inquire how he was getting along.

"Oh, I never did have that operation," he said. "The doctors decided that they must have made a mistake in the diagnosis. My headaches completely left me and I don't reel anymore. In fact, I never felt better in my life!"

As I hung up the receiver I was hearing again in my mind the promise, *Again I say unto you, That if two of you shall agree on earth as touching anything that they shall ask, it shall be done for them of my Father which is in heaven.*

There have been so many healings. I hear of them so often that I am no longer surprised. There are bones that knit together so rapidly that the doctors can hardly believe it. I have known of every kind of healing including various cases of terminal cancer.

One time at a series of healing meetings we had this experience. One of the prayer requests was for a woman who was not present. The request simply said, "Stomach." Now, I don't know anything about stomachs, *per se*, but I figure that the infinite Intelligence that created them knows all that needs to be known. I remember that I treated to know that this person was a divine, perfect, spiritual being who had never been contaminated by any disorder; that she was one with the perfect Life of God; that this perfect Life lived through her now. Everyone at the meeting joined in that treatment. There was a tremendous healing consciousness in the room that night. I think that before we got through everyone there was convinced that there was nothing to heal, that the woman was already whole and perfect.

The next morning Mrs. Addington received a call from the person who had made the request. The woman was thrilled. She told Mrs. Addington that she had had chronic hepatitis for a number of years. She had been nauseated for so long that she despaired of ever feeling well again. She said that she had become thoroughly discouraged, but that as of eight o'clock the previous evening (the exact time of our prayer treatment) she felt wonderful! She just wasn't sick anymore at all. As of today the healing still stands. Does this surprise you? The Master Teacher said, *It is done unto you as you believe.*

In these healings that I have recounted, there was in each instance:

1. a desire to be healed
2. a belief in the Power of God
3. an acceptance of the healing

Spirit transcends the laws of the material world and the world calls it a miracle. I firmly believe that there is nothing impossible to the Almighty Power of God within us right now. Know often for yourself:

> There is no power in conditions
> There is no power in situations
> There is only power in God;
>     Almighty God within me right now.
> There is no person, place, thing, condition,
>     or circumstance that can interfere with
>     the perfect right action of God Almighty
>     within me right now.[4]

[4] Jack and Cornelia Addington, *Your Needs Met.*

# EIGHT

## There Are No Incurable Diseases When You Understand the Creative Law

*With men this is impossible; but with God all things are possible.*—Matthew 19:26

The late Dr. Frederick Bailes, author of *Your Mind Can Heal You* and *Hidden Power for Human Problems,*[1] was a very good friend of mine. One time he sat in my study and told me a most interesting story about himself.

As a young man he went to London to study to be a medical missionary. He had finished his ministerial studies and was embarking on medicine when competent medical authorities told him that he had diabetes, a supposedly incurable malady. Dr. Banting had not yet given insulin to the world. He was advised that on a careful diet he might live eighteen months. Fred told me that he was miserably confused. How could this be? Hadn't his im-

[1] Frederick Bailes, *Your Mind Can Heal You* (New York: Dodd, Mead & Co., 1971); *Hidden Power For Human Problems* (Englewood Cliffs, N.J.: Prentice Hall, Inc., 1957).

117

portant years been given to getting ready for God's service? Hadn't he dedicated his life to helping mankind? He could not understand why God wasn't on his side; he was a medical missionary student.

"I wasn't just a grind. I'd led a healthy life," Fred said. "Coming from New Zealand, I had been an athlete—golf, bicycle racing, boxing, wrestling, swimming, tennis, cricket, hunting, and fishing—I loved life. I wanted desperately to live. Why did this have to happen to me?"

I remember so well our conversation. One thing Fred emphasized to me was that even though he had been given an ultimatum by the medical doctors, he just could not and would not believe it. Bear in mind that at that time a diagnosis of diabetes was considered to be just as final as terminal cancer is today.

## A Discovery That Changed His Life

Not long after he had been given this death sentence he picked up a book at a friend's house and began to browse through it. He became fascinated with its contents. What was in this book changed the course of his life. The book was *The Creative Process in the Individual* by Judge Thomas Troward,[2] an Englishman, a devout churchman, who had served as a judge in India and was a great student of comparative religions, having studied the religions of the East. This book, while not on healing, brought out the Universal Principle that takes men's desires, hopes, and choices, and manifests them as form. Troward called it *The Creative Process.*

Fred's eyes shone as he told me how excited he was,

2 Thomas Troward, *The Creative Process in the Individual,* rev. ed. (New York: Dodd, Mead & Co., Inc., 1952. London: L. N. Fowler & Co., Ltd., 1956).

particularly in the face of his problem, to discover that the Judge believed that every thought became manifest into form.

"Judge Troward was so logical in a judicial way," Fred said. "Just like a lawyer, he built a case to prove his assertion that any one of us can bring into his life his choices through the Infinite Creative Process operating through the mind of the individual.

"At first," he said, "I didn't go along with everything that Troward said. After all, I was of a very orthodox sect and I shrank from many of Troward's unorthodox statements. However, my need was great and the promise held out to me was just like a reprieve from a death sentence. I wanted to live and so I studied on for nearly two years, completely engrossed in the writings of Thomas Troward.

"I didn't receive my healing at once. The results were not striking, but gradually I recovered. The tests showed after some weeks that the pancreas was beginning to awake from its lethargy. From then on the course of improvement was definite."

### A Victorious Treatment

At the end of eighteen months Fred Bailes was far from dead. However, though he continued to improve, at the end of six years he was not completely healed. There was still a trace of sugar. Telling about this period in his life, he wrote:

One evening I sat with elbows on desk, head on hands, eyes closed. Then I started, quietly and confidently, to declare something like this: "Whatever is blocking my complete recovery must be some hidden strand of thought that holds some mental reservation. I am not aware of its nature, where it started, or what keeps it active. But it must be mine, whether I can trace my way to it or not.

"I do not want it to keep operating, therefore I now declare that it is a vestige of my former destructive thought. I emphatically state that it is completely out of line with the Infinite Thinker's thoughts which are trying to manifest perfectly through me. It is a squatter living on territory where it has no rights of any sort. I call in the law to evict, dissolve, and negate it *right now*.

"I wash my hands of it. I do not have to fight it, worry about it, or pay any attention to it. It is nothing trying to be something. It is no more real than the bogey man that scared me as a boy. I turn every last thread of my thought to the contemplation of that steady movement of the thought of God in me and through every single cell of my body.

"I think of Its beauty, Its unutterable harmonies, Its total unawareness of any resisting force, Its breathing of 'It is good' as It contemplates the universe It has brought into being. Quietly now I let myself drift into the innermost parts of that Infinite Mind, catch something of Its unshakeable peace, knowing that this Mind flows through me as my mind."

I went on affirming the power of the Infinite and Its perfect image of my body, concluding by expressing my gratitude for the healing that I declared was taking place. My last words were the customary ones, "It *is* so."

I got up, went out, and walked along the bank of the Rock River in Wisconsin. I looked at the stars, trees, and river; quietly I said, "They are good, all good; for they too are ideas held by God."

The next laboratory report said, "Sugar negative." It was so. It has never returned.[3]

## A Principle Not Confined to the Healing of the Body

In more than fifty years following his dramatic healing Dr. Bailes had occasion to use this principle in many areas.

[3] Bailes, *Hidden Power for Human Problems.*

He found that it could be applied to any situation. The same law worked in the business world. He found that it was the same principle by which food, securities, automobiles, or real estate could be successfully sold. It can draw love into a person's life and enable him to pass difficult examinations. IIe used it to bring harmony in chaotic situations. It is the one universal principle, he found, by which one can bring into his life anything he desires without hurting others. In short, Dr. Bailes used the Creative Law throughout the rest of his life and by all the world's standards he was highly successful. More than that, he found peace of mind and complete fulfillment in his life. His radio program, "Peace in a Changing World" reached millions of ears and changed many lives. His popular books are read and circulated throughout the world.

Dr. Bailes states the Creative Law in a capsule statement:

A simple statement of Creative Law would be that man lives in a surrounding River of Mind, into which his thoughts fall, and which ceaselessly turns all these thoughts into form. The River seems to obey man, because Its nature is to translate his thoughts into experience. Its power is limitless; Its knowledge of ways and means is infinite; Its willingness to produce is without the slightest reservation. It is the working side of the Eternal God.[4]

### Thought Itself Is Not the Power

So much has been said about the power of positive thinking that it may come as a shock to many to hear that thought is *not* the Power, thought only channels the Power.

4 Ibid.

Dr. Norman Vincent Peale, the famous minister of Marble Collegiate Church in New York, wrote a book entitled the *Power of Positive Thinking.*[5] It is an excellent book which has helped thousands of people straighten out their thinking and get in tune with life.

Another fine book which everyone should read is *Power Through Constructive Thinking* by Dr. Emmet Fox.[6] We have all spoken of the power of thought, the power of imagination, the power of prayer; but, actually, while thought may seem to be a power, there is only One Power. Thought releases the Power into our lives; thought is the mental mold that we prepare for the Power to work in and through us. Positive thinking opens the door and lets the Power come in. Just as Dr. Bailes's positive treatment prepared the way for his healing, our positive, affirmative thoughts prepare the way for the Power to go to work in our lives.

In her book, *The Healing Light,* Agnes Sanford puts it this way:

When our electric lights work partially or not at all, we know that the lack of power is not in the universal and infinite and eternal flow of electricity in the universe, but in the wiring that connects us with that flow.[7]

We have all had the experience of having an electric light bulb burn out. When we do, we replace it with a new one, never doubting for a moment that the source will supply us with light. We know that it was our connec-

---

[5] Norman Vincent Peale, *Power of Positive Thinking* (Englewood Cliffs, N.J.: Prentice Hall, 1952).
[6] Emmet Fox, *Power Through Constructive Thinking.*
[7] Agnes Sanford, *The Healing Light,* p. 25, (St. Paul, Minnesota: Macalester Park Publishing Company, 1947).

tion that was bad and do not blame the power of electricity. In the experience of living, individual thought is the connection to Universal Mind. As Emerson said, each man is an inlet and an outlet of the One Mind at his point of awareness.

In order to clarify our thinking we must start with the premise: There is only one Power, the Power of Almighty God. Every time we think, whatever the thought may be, positive or negative, we are forming a mental mold and the Power, always available, flows into that mold.

When you do your treatment work (scientific prayer work), you, yourself, do not heal anyone, but, through your thought processes, you create a mold for healing.

The late Dr. Glenn Clark, in describing this invisible thing, wrote:

In Northern Siberia there is a Russian port, used for whaling vessels in the summer season. But in winter with the temperatures ranging from fifty to ninety degrees below zero, no vessels have ever been known to enter. The port is there, the wharves are there, all the avenues for ships to come and go are there. But no vessels ever come. It would be silly to ask why because everyone knows why they don't come in. It is because of the wrong kind of climate.

Anyone who steps into the presence of Agnes [Sanford] steps into the right kind of climate for healing.[8]

## All Have Access to the Power

If God is the only Power, why is it that some are able to invoke the healing Power and others fail? Have you ever wondered that so few are considered healers and

8 Sanford, *The Healing Light*, Introduction.

others seem unable to make contact? What is the secret? It is very simple: We all have access to the Power. When we become in tune with it we become good conductors and can be considered instruments of healing. Affirmative thinking is not itself the Power, but it is very important because it is through our thinking that we are able to build a mold through which the Power can express Itself in our lives. The Power is willing but we must direct It through the choices we make. It says to us: *Ask and you shall receive.*

I think that this is very important because oftentimes people become superstitious about their thinking. Having seen the results of negative thinking, they get the idea that their lives depend upon their thoughts and the next step is to assume that they can think things into being. The result is a process of mental manipulation that gets them into all kinds of trouble.

Another pitfall in the "thought is power" school is worrying about past negative thinking. Some people become so bogged down in stewing about their old negative thought patterns that they have little time or energy left to set up new affirmative patterns.

So, we must ask ourselves, is negative thinking a power? The answer is: No, negative thinking is not a power either. Negative thinking only has the power that we give it. What can we do to get rid of old patterns of negative thinking? A good plan is to take the time to make a list of our old negative thoughts, those fears and doubts and self-imposed limitations. Imagine that each one is written on a very fragile piece of china and then mentally drop each one on the floor and break it. You can break those old flimsy molds of negative thinking just as easily as that, and then there will be no possible way for them to affect your experience ever again. When we think of thought as power we create a new ogre and give it dominion over us. If thought were power we would be stuck with all those old negative thoughts we've harbored for so long. Thank goodness, this is not the case. We can break those old mental molds just as easily as we can break a china cup.

Affirmations and denials help us break the old molds and create new ones. Affirm daily:

> There is no power in thought, my own or anyone else's.
> I refuse to give room to negative thoughts and suggestions.
> I now establish new affirmative molds of thought.
> I affirm that I am free from past mistakes and all unproductive thinking.
> I choose to think thoughts of life, thoughts of good, thoughts of divine right action.

Now reverse any specific negative thoughts and list them in the affirmative. For instance, if you have thought of yourself as ill, tired, miserable, lonely, and unsuccessful, claim:

> I am strong with the strength of the almighty.
> I am whole with the health of perfect life.
> Love surrounds me and keeps me. I am never alone.
> Through the power of God I succeed in all that I do.

The best way to break those old thought molds is through meditation and scientific prayer. Through scientific prayer we clarify our thinking. *Let that mind be in you, which was also in Christ Jesus,* Paul advised. What is that mind that he asks us to have? The Christ Consciousness is Oneness with the Father. Dr. Ernest Holmes once said to me: "Anything that comes between you and your God is a false god. Get rid of it." Through prayer we get rid of those old false gods which have tried to come between us and our awareness of the Presence and Power of God in our lives. It has been said that there is only one sickness, a sense of separation from divine and perfect Life.

## New Mental Molds Produce New Experiences for Us

It is not surprising that when this changing of the mind takes place our bodies begin to reflect the change and we say that we have had a healing.

A friend of ours is a good example. For many years she had felt rejected by life and this made her very lonely and unhappy. Then she learned about scientific prayer. She learned that through prayer she could put herself in harmony with life. Whereas, formerly, she had prayed to a God afar off which only served to make her feel even lonelier, now she learned to pray in such a way that she experienced the Presence of Love right where she was. She became immersed in it. Little by little, the old lonely feelings of rejection began to fall away. She became so completely changed in her inner life that her friends hardly knew her. "What has happened to you?" they asked her. Before, she had been a drab, gloomy sort of person. Now she was radiant. She felt loved and so everyone loved her. But that wasn't all that happened to her when she learned how to pray. She had several physical healings that came as a surprise to her. She told me that they seemed to be by-products of her other blessings. You see, she hadn't prayed for the physical healings, they came about as her thinking changed. She changed those thought molds and mental and physical changes were the result.

For instance, she said that she had had severe hay fever. Every summer she had to go away during the hay fever season. All year long she took shots for her allergies. Some years her hay fever got so bad that she had such a lot of trouble breathing that she had to sit up all night just to breathe and as she got progressively worse the hay fever developed into asthma. She said she didn't mind too much having to sit up all night as she had insomnia anyway. I took it that she had become so used to her problem that she no longer resisted it. It seems she also had chronic eczema, and this annoyed her most of all. Her throat and chest, she said, had for years been covered with little unsightly blisters and itched until she thought that she would go mad. For years she had gone to doctors and doctored the condition herself with various lotions, but had found no relief for the annoying condition. She told me that the healings of these ailments came so easily, so gradually, that she wasn't aware of them at the time. She just forgot that she had ever had these problems! And then, one day about two years later, she remembered all of a sudden. "I don't have hay fever any more!" She checked back and found that it had been over two years since she had had a hay fever shot.

"Let's see," she thought, "what other problems did I use to have?" That was when she remembered that she used to have that old itchy skin. She felt her throat and chest and found that it was as smooth as a baby's skin.

And she couldn't remember when she had had trouble sleeping. These healings had come so effortlessly that she had not been aware they were taking place. "They just came when I wasn't looking!" she said.

She had become so absorbed in the mental metamorphosis that was taking place that she forgot all about her physical problems that had formerly been so important. Through scientific prayer she had changed her thinking; she had broken the old negative thought molds. *Be ye transformed by the renewing of your mind.*[9] That is just what happened. She was transformed spiritually, mentally, and physically.

Dr. Bailes had been told that there was no cure for diabetes. The woman of whom we were just speaking had been told that she would have hay fever the rest of her life. Both were healed through the changing of the mind. The River of Life flowed in and filled the new thought molds and they were made whole. These are not unusual cases. It happens daily. This is the Creative Law at work. Spirit, working through Mind, is the Creator.

THERE ARE NO INCURABLE DISEASES

> *Let this mind be in you which was also in Christ Jesus.*
> —Philippians 2:5

In the One Mind there are no incurable diseases; there is only the perfection of God. In the One Life there are no dangerous symptoms, difficult conditions, no pain or suffering. The awareness of the Presence of God dissolves these troublesome thoughts and their seeming effects as "a Light shining in a dark place." The Christ Mind is the Mind of God, the con-

9 Romans 12:2.

sciousness that "all Power is given unto me in heaven (within) and earth (without)" and "I and my Father are one." As I let this mind be in me I am clothed in shining garments (spiritual thoughts) of perfection. I speak the healing word of God with the authority of the Christ. God's perfection is my perfection and shines on all that I behold. "That Light that lighteth every man" illumines my world and the universe. There is only *one life*, the Life of God. That Life has never been sick, never suffered, never been less than Whole. That Life is my life and the life of my loved one. All is well.

And so it is.

# NINE

## The Prayer That Is Always Answered

*Prayer is not the overcoming of God's reluctance,*
*but the taking hold of God's willingness.*—Phillips Brooks

How glibly we say: "Nothing shall be impossible to God,"
and yet some of us go right on having what we call "un-
answered prayers." We say that nothing is impossible to
God, but do we really believe it? I wonder how many of
us really expect our prayers to be fulfilled.

I love the story of the preacher who was walking home
from his church one day when he passed three boys changing a tire. The boys were arguing and struggling with the
tire and with each other.

The preacher stopped, smiled benignly at the boys, and
said: "Now, this will never do."

"Well, what would you do?" one of the boys asked de-
fiantly.

"I would stop for a few moments and pray," the minister offered.

The boys stopped everything and their spokesman said:
"All right, pray."

So the minister prayed and while he was praying the tire automatically changed itself. Yes, the car jacked itself up and the tire slipped into place and was changed so that when the prayer was finished they all looked and sure enough the thing was done.

The minister scratched his head and with a puzzled expression said: "Well, I'll be darned!"

All too often we are like the congregation that held a special service to pray for rain. There was only one person, a little girl, who brought an umbrella.

## What About Unanswered Prayer

What would you do if you were sick in bed and Jesus came to your bedside and told you to *take up your bed and walk?* Would you believe you were healed, or would you say, "I can't, I'm sick in bed." If he told you that you were healed, would you say, "I hope so. I've been sick such a long time. How I've suffered. You'll never know how miserable I've been!"

Prayer is always answered if and when we are able to accept the answer. It is not that God takes a long time over the healing, but that we take such a long time reaching the place where we can receive it. It takes us so long to convince ourselves that we have been healed. So we must ask ourselves, "Are we praying beyond our beliefs? Are we praying because prayer is such a lot of pretty words put together? Or, are we using scientific prayer for the purpose of realizing a radical change in our experience?" All too often we pray, "Change my life but don't change me." I remember Ernest Holmes often said, "People want to be

healed of their neuroses but do not want to give them up."
Unfortunately, the change is not something that happens
*out there,* the change must occur in the area of our beliefs.

I remember hearing a friend of mine give a beautiful
treatment aloud for her mother. She had the words but
not the "music." As we left the sickroom, she remarked
unthinkingly, "This is the end for mother." And then she
recited all of the symptoms again, the doctor's diagnosis
and prognosis, just as if she had never had a spiritual mind
treatment for her mother.

## The Healing of Naaman Points the Way

Possibly you've never heard of Naaman for he is not a
prominent character as Bible characters go. Naaman, the
Bible tells us, was a great man, *a mighty man in valour.*
He was a captain in the Syrian army; in fact, through him
the Lord had delivered Syria. Naaman was close to the
king, respected by the king and by the people. But Naaman was a leper. Now among the prisoners whom the
Syrians had taken out of Israel was a little maid who
waited on Naaman's wife. She couldn't help remarking
to her mistress that she wished that Naaman were with
the prophet in Samaria for then he would be healed of his
leprosy.

Word of this got back to the king of Syria. Now there
was nothing the king wouldn't do to help Naaman, so he
sent a messenger with a letter and gifts of gold and silver
to the king of Israel, asking that the king heal Naaman
of his leprosy.

The king of Israel *tore his hair and rent his garments,*

the Bible says. He thought this was a trap, that the Syrian king was trying to provoke a quarrel with him, for how could he heal anyone?

But Elisha heard about the matter. Elisha's name (nature) means "God is savior." So Elisha said to the king: *Wherefore hast thou rent thy clothes? Let him come now to me.* So Naaman came with his horses and his chariot and stood at Elisha's door. But, instead of coming out to meet the great Syrian captain, Elisha sent a message to him that if he would wash in the Jordan seven times he would be clean. This was an insult to Naaman. Naaman was proud and he wasn't about to sacrifice any of his pride. "What?" said Naaman, "We've got better rivers in Syria! Why shouldn't I wash myself in those rivers?"

Naaman thought that surely Elisha would come out to him and call upon the name of his God and heal him. He was so angry that he went away in a rage. He must not have known that the river Jordan is the symbol of the River of Life and that seven is the mystical number that means wholeness and completeness. Seven in the Bible is the mystical number denoting something that is finished, complete, perfection, release.[1] Elisha had offered Naaman an act of faith, but Naaman had to protect his pride. So, in a great rage, he gathered his men together and left in his impressive chariot for home. It reminds me of the verse in the Psalms: *Some trust in chariots, and some in horses: but we will remember the name of the Lord our God.*[2] Naaman, at that point, wasn't ready to sacrifice his pride and place his reliance on God.

---

[1] See Jack Ensign Addington, *Hidden Mystery of the Bible.*
[2] Psalms 20:7.

But, on the way home one of his servants remarked: "Master, if the prophet had asked you to do some difficult thing, wouldn't you have done it? Wouldn't you rather, then, that he tell you to wash and be clean?"

Apparently Naaman had not thought of it that way, for he turned around and, putting aside his pride, dipped himself in the Jordan seven times and the Bible reports, *His Flesh came again like unto the flesh of a little child, and he was clean.* He returned and showed himself to Elisha. It took perserverance and discipline. Seven times he had dipped himself in the Jordan signifying complete immersion in the Life of the Spirit. Then he was cleansed.[3] There is a great lesson here. How many of us are willing to be teachable, to forsake our prideful attitudes and hypocritical beliefs? To immerse ourselves completely in the Spirit?

### Who Did Hinder You?

*Ye did run well; who did hinder you that ye should not obey the truth?* [4] wrote the apostle Paul to the Galatians. What is it that is hindering us from receiving the answer to our prayer? We pray for perfect health and then continue to accept our old foolish beliefs about ourselves, convinced that our health depends upon certain medical attention, placing our faith upon this and that, or, making excuses for our state in an endless round of judgment by appearances. We know, deep within us, that our hostile

3 II Kings 5:1-14.            4 Galatians 5:7.

and antagonistic thoughts have brought about our downfall, yet we continue to hang on to them for dear life. "Change my life but don't change me!" is still our cry as we carefully guard our secret hates and fears, our guilts and resistances, letting them burrow deeper and ever deeper into the subconscious. *Who did hinder you?* Only *you* can hinder you. You, yourself, must become the answer to your prayer. There is nothing superstitious about this. Mind is everywhere present, expressing in every part of life. The Divine Life has never been less than perfect. *Ye ask and receive not,* said James, *because ye ask amiss.* How do we ask amiss? By not being ready to follow through and be the demonstration. Many conscientious souls have prayed for years, futilely wondering why their prayers were never answered. Let me pose some questions:

1. What neurotic pattern would you rather live with than accept the answered prayer?

2. What person would you rather continue to hate than have the answer to your prayer?

3. Has your sickness provided a means of getting attention? of getting what substitutes (poorly) for love from the members of your family?

4. Do you wallow in self-pity and need your symptoms to perpetuate that self-pity?

You must make the choice. What is important to you? Naaman had pride. Pride delayed his healing. Often pride keeps us from our good. We have to be willing to admit that our thinking has not been sound. We have to admit that we have made a mistake and that we are ready to start over again. And then, we must forgive the past and wipe it out of our consciousness. Naaman resisted spiritual discipline. He was angry for awhile until he saw his mistake. It is all so simple—too simple—once we see the Light. *Who did hinder you?* It is always the Truth that sets us free. If your healing has been slow in coming, if the answers seem to remain hidden from you, pray that you may know the Truth, that particular Truth that you need to know and so be set free.

In Chapter Ten we will investigate other hindrances to answered prayer.


## Is There an Explanation for Failure in Healing?

Even Jesus was not always able to heal the people. We are told that his work was not effective in Nazareth, his home town. There he was just the carpenter's son and the people, we are told, were offended that he should set himself up as a healer.

One day Jesus was walking along the road when he came upon a crowd of people surrounding his disciples and the scribes were questioning them. It seemed that a father had brought his son to the disciples for them to heal him. The father turned to Jesus and said: "I have asked your disciples to heal my son. He has seizures, he falls into the water and into the fire and he is in a very bad condition."

And Jesus commanded the dumb spirit to come out of the boy and he was healed.

The disciples couldn't wait to get into the house away from the crowd where they could ask Jesus privately why it was that their work was not effective. And he told them,

*This kind can come forth by nothing, but by prayer and fasting.*[5] The disciples had accepted the condition as real. The appearances were so convincing that they had accepted them as something that could not be healed, what we might call today an incurable disease. Jesus recognized that it takes fasting from the negative belief. He had schooled himself to turn away from the condition. He knew that he and the Father were One which means that divine Wholeness is everywhere present.

There is no question about it, there are cases that seem to present more of a challenge to us than others; but only because we have allowed ourselves to be taken in by the appearances. To God there is no great or small. The problem lies in our unbelief. Divine Perfection knows only Itself. The only reality is divine Life, perfect, whole, complete, omnipresent. *This kind can come forth by nothing, but by prayer and fasting.*

When you are tempted to be overcome by the appearances of sickness and disaster remember the boy with the dumb spirit. He put on a most convincing show of symptoms, he fell on the ground, foamed at the mouth, gnashed his teeth. So convincing was the spectacle that even the disciples were taken in by the appearances. When you are confronted by a situation that seems incurable, face it strongly and declare:

THERE IS ONLY ONE POWER AND THAT POWER IS GOD

THERE IS ONLY ONE LIFE AND THAT LIFE IS THE LIFE OF GOD.

THEREFORE THERE IS NO POWER IN APPEARANCES

THERE IS NO POWER IN CONDITIONS

THERE IS NO POWER IN CIRCUMSTANCES

5 Mark 9:29.

**THERE IS NO POWER IN DISEASE**
**THERE IS ONLY POWER IN GOD, ALMIGHTY GOD WITHIN ME**
**RIGHT NOW.**

**And so it is.**

# TEN

## What Did Hinder You?

*Stand fast therefore in the liberty wherewith Christ hath made us free, and be not entangled again with the yoke of bondage. Ye did run well; who did hinder you that ye should not obey the TRUTH.*—9 Galatians 5:1, 7

"When I pray for others they seem to get answers, but when I pray for myself it just doesn't seem to work for me."

"What's wrong with me that *my* prayers are never answered?"

"I never seem to get through to God."

"I used to feel that I made contact with God, but I just don't seem to anymore."

How often I have heard these words! What did hinder these people that their prayers seemed to be blocked? In looking through my correspondence I find that the above remarks are usually followed by some highly revealing statements, statements that indicate stumbling blocks to answered prayer. In this chapter I propose to discuss some of these stumbling blocks.

## *Why Some Prayers Are Stillborn*

People whose prayers are never answered, far from being discriminated against, are people whose minds are so filled with human judgments about themselves and others that they are unable to listen to the Father in secret and cannot receive the reward that is there for them, the reward that will come openly. Many people are so stubborn that they insist that their prayers be answered the way they want them to be answered.

When we enter our mental closet leaving outside the problems, the fears, and the anxieties, we should be able, if we have prayed aright, to walk out of that closet completely free. The problems should not be waiting outside of the door for us. They should have dissolved into their native nothingness. Problems are not real; they have only the power we ascribe to them. We know when we have prayed aright, for the peace that passeth all understanding comes into our hearts. If we continue to worry and feel anxious we can be sure it is because we have continued to hang onto our negative thoughts. This is what Jesus meant by putting new wine into old bottles. We are always trying to superimpose the answer onto the problem without letting go of the problem. It is like trying to see the beauty of the day while looking through a very dirty window. As I write this I am sitting beside a window that is streaked with mud after yesterday's storm. Outside the air is fresh and clean. I am amazed when I go outside to find a sparkling day. Had I continued to look through my dirty window I would have missed it all.

*Your Secret Referent*

Through whose eyes are you looking at life? Who is your secret referent. A son greatly admires his father who happens to be a very critical person. The son fails to please his father. Nothing he does satisfies this very critical man. Pleasing the father image becomes an obsession with the son. All through his life, and long after the father has passed on, the son is subconsciously asking, "Is this the way father would have done it? Would this have pleased my father?" Finally, he becomes as critical as his father because he sees everything through his father's eyes. No matter what life gives him, he is never pleased. His prayers are never answered and will never be answered until he is able to be true to himself. His stumbling block is his feeling about his father.

As Polonius advised Laertes in *Hamlet*, "This above all: to thine own self be true, and it must follow, as the night the day, thou canst not then be false to any man." You'd be surprised how many of us separate ourselves from our good by judging our lives through the eyes of a secret referent.

A woman I know nearly wrecked her life because she was a compulsive perfectionist. Everything in her life had to be perfect. Everything she purchased had to be ultimate perfection. To her, shopping was agony. What if she bought the wrong thing? What if she failed to find the perfect article? "As sterling is to silver," she used to say. No compromise was acceptable. Her house was immaculate and every room ready at all times to be pictured in *House Beautiful*. It did not matter whether she was entertaining or not; the flower arrangements were artistic perfection; there was never a magazine out of place. And her dinners! The table was a picture, the service as perfect as if she had had a house full of servants. No event could be spontaneous, it had to be planned, usually through long sleepless nights, and executed with precision. The strain of it all showed on her face, and heaven help the person who failed to do his part exactly as she wanted it done. She was never satisfied with her life or the results of her efforts. She complained bitterly that her prayers were never answered. Nothing pleased her. Why? She saw everything through the eyes of Aunt Martha, another perfectionist of the first water. Her dominant thought was, "What would Aunt Martha think?"

Finally, there came a crisis in her life. In her prayers she asked for help. Her answer came. The Truth, at first, was painful. Finally she was able to give up this obsession with Aunt Martha and live her own life. Her life changed. She became a relaxed and charming person, fulfilled in her own right and pleased with the answers to her prayers. She learned to meet life spontaneously, living moment by moment wtihout anxiety but with a sense of serenity. To the best of my knowledge she lived easily and happily ever after.

## Inability to Forgive Is a Hindrance

The more I see of life, the more I realize that one of the great hindrances to answered prayer is our inability to forgive. Jesus touched on this in the Lord's Prayer. *Forgive us our trespasses as we forgive those who trespass against us.* He understood how grudges and condemnation could hinder the free flow of the spirit within man. Psychologists understand the importance of eliminating grudges, self-condemnation, and condemnation of others. It is a very important part of their therapy to eliminate this kind of thinking in order that the patient may understand his own relationship to life.

Once we understand forgiveness, we are able to harvest the fruits of our prayers. Until we do understand forgiveness and learn to forgive with just as much precision and persistence as we used in holding the grudge, our lives will be filled with unhappiness and our prayers will fail.

## You Have To Do Something About It

Forgiveness takes an overt act on our part. In other words, we have to do something about it. Forgiveness is far from being automatic. It takes effort and it takes ability to forgive. In the first place, we must want to forgive.

"I want to forgive her but I just can't!"

"How can I forgive him after what he did to me?"

"Someday I might be able to forgive him. I'm working at it!"

Sound familiar? We've probably all entertained thoughts like these. Wanting to forgive precedes forgiveness. We must persist until the mind is free.

## What Does Forgiveness Mean?

Forgiveness means to give up any feeling against; to give up resentment against; to give up any hate against; to give up condemnation. The feeling can be against some other person, or it can be against one's self, or it can be against God.

Often in their prayers, people think, "God, why did this have to happen to me?" This brings in a sense of resentment against God for letting the thing happen. Of course, this is foolishness. Actually, God has never done anything against us. God is Omnipresent. How can any part of the Infinite be against Itself? Man, being made in the image and likeness of God, is one with the Presence of God. Therefore, in truth there is no way for man to be against God, or for God to be against man. Whenever man holds anything against God, or thinks that God holds anything against him, it is not the truth. Such thinking causes a sense of separation from God.

## Do You Hinder Your Own Growth?

Another reason that forgiveness is so important is that if we hold a grudge against someone, we hold it against ourselves. *Who did hinder thee?* What is wrong with your prayers? Why aren't your prayers answered? Ask yourself the question, "Who is hindering me?" Jesus answered this for us when he said *If it should happen that while you are presenting your offering upon the altar, and right there you remember that your brother has any grievance against you, leave your offering there upon the altar, and first go and make peace with your brother, and then come back and present your offering.*[1] Our offering is our treatment.

1 Matthew 5:23, 24.

and as long as we are entertaining any sense of unrest or conflict with our brother, it is certain that this feeling will interfere with it. We should mentally go and make peace with the brother. Then the mind becomes clarified and ready for the treatment.

Before we do our treatment work, we should think with sincerity and with an inward feeling of believing and knowing, "I forgive each and every person that I have ever had anything against in my life. I forgive each and every person who has ever had anything against me. I am one with all of life. I love all of life. I love the life of God within me and within my fellow man." Now there exists a feeling of divine unity, a recognition of the omnipresence of life that is so essential to good treatment work. By doing this, we forgive ourselves and we forgive others.

### Forgiving Is Not Forgetting

One day a woman came to me and asked me the question point-blank, "How can I forgive my ex-husband who abandoned me and then took the children away from me through lying and was able to steal all of the property that we had accumulated during our married life?" My answer was a further question to her, "How can you afford not to forgive him? By holding resentment, you are destroying only yourself."

When we forgive, we do not condone what the other person did, but we look beyond this and recognize the truth of his being. There is no justification whatsoever in holding anything against anyone, or in holding anything against the self. Man is continually setting up reasons why certain things cannot be forgiven. I think that this is due to the old saying of forgive and forget. I have heard many people say, "Oh, just forget it and you will be able to forgive." That's not the answer. In the first place, you cannot forget—the more you try to forget, the more you will hang on to it. Forgiving has to come through releasing. If there is any animosity or antagonism or grudge, then it is impossible to forgive, for there is no way to release until there is a clarification.

But, even so, there is no forgetting. Why? Because we have a little tape recorder right within the mind that is constantly at work. This recorder tapes all of the pictures and all of the words that go with them, and keeps them very carefully tucked away. Have you ever come across a diary of some twenty or thirty years ago? You read along and all of a sudden, you find that your mind has not forgotten. You were surprised that you could recall it. Once you began to have something to associate with that period, you found the recall was there. While we do not forget, we can change our reactions to past events and past thinking. When we forgive, we are neutralizing all negative and antagonistic thinking about the past event. Now, it has no power over us.

*Forgiveness Is a Practical Way*

In the book *The Miracle of Mind Power* [2] by the late Dr. Dan Custer there is an excellent story on forgiveness. Dr. Custer tells of a man who was a failure in business.

[2] Dan Custer, *The Miracle of Mind Power* (Englewood Cliffs, N.J.: Prentice Hall, Inc., 1960).

Twenty-eight years before he had been in a very successful business with a partner, and the partner stole from the firm causing the firm to go broke. This man felt thoroughly justified in hating the crooked partner. He carried this grudge for twenty-eight years, unable to do creative work because during all of that period he was thinking about that partner and the dirty thing he did. When it was pointed out to him that he was only hurting himself by this kind of thinking, and that he had to forgive his partner by truly loving him, he, at first, revolted against this idea. But he began to see that there was no other salvation. So he did forgive the partner. He changed his whole feeling about him, tried to understand the partner, to realize that he, too, had suffered a great deal through this mistake. He truly developed a feeling of understanding for his partner. From that moment on, he succeeded again in becoming a successful and well-balanced person.

## Importance of Love

Much is said today about the importance of love, but the big question is, how can we learn to love? We learn to love by learning love techniques. One of the most important is the forgiveness technique: forgive yourself, forgive others, and forgive God. Right away several questions come to mind. Why should we forgive when it's so much fun to have a grudge? Why forgive when someone has done to you what seems to be an irreparable wrong? We must forgive because without forgiveness there can be no love. Forgiveness *must* precede love. Forgiveness is giving up resentment, hate, or any such feelings that are contrary to the feeling of love. Forgiveness opens the way for clarity of thinking, for sensible thinking. Love can now come into the picture.

When two people get together to "run down" another, there is low-grade hate at work. Some people think that it is natural to gossip about others, but gossip is resentment in which two people are in common agreement. It seems to be a natural thing, but really, love is the natural thing. Sometimes it builds the ego to find someone worse than we are. In reading the newspaper we are continually setting ourselves up as being "good" in comparison to others who are doing "foul deeds." Again, hate is running rampant. We love only when we are able to recognize the good in others, to affirm the good, and to love the good. When we do this, we are able to overlook the bad and not give power to that which seems to be evil.

### Paul's Positive Thinking Message

In Paul's letter to the Philippians, he said, *Whatsoever things are true, whatsoever things are honest, whatsoever things are just, whatsoever things are pure, whatsoever things are lovely, whatsoever things are of good report; if there be any virtue, and if there be any praise, think on these things.* It is interesting that the foregoing is followed by this statement: *And the God of peace shall be with you.*[3]

Let your conversation be in heaven. Whenever we have something to say about another, if it isn't in accord with Paul's admonition, then it is better unsaid. We will have

3 Philippians 4:8, 9.

less to forgive ourselves for. Guilt is dependent upon condemnation of the self. When we feel guilty we are condemning the self. When we condemn others, we also condemn ourselves. This is the reason we feel out of harmony with life after we have indulged in a gossip session, or when we have spent time maligning another, accusing him in our hearts. Nothing is going to be gained by condemning others. The only one hurt is the one who does the condemning.

## Forgiveness and Peace of Mind

Why forgive? It is imperative that we forgive if we want to have peace of mind. Hate is like a bonfire; it scorches the ground upon which it burns. Hate hardens the heart in which it is allowed to rest. Hate interferes with creativity. It blocks the ability to think clearly and causes good thoughts to go out the window. *Perfect Love casteth out fear.*[4] Perfect Love is the Love we have when we are affirming and respecting the Life within us, the Life within others.

This is what I call loving God. Perfect Love casts out not only fear, but all of the children of fear: resentment, anxiety, hostility, jealousy, bitterness, and greed. Anger is fear that has lost its anchor. Anger stems out of frustration. Frustration results from fear that one is not living his best life and doing the things he would like to do. Frustration is bondage to a condition. Do you know why we cannot afford to find fault, to hate, and to hold resentment against others? Because hatred, resentment, anger, anguish,

[4] I John 4:18.

criticism, condemnation, and judgments separate us from Love. They also make us mentally and physically ill.

## Why Love?

Love is a necessary ingredient to a happy, successful, joyous, creative and productive life. Love is more important than knowledge. Love is more important than wealth. Love will bring happiness and fulfillment into our experience as nothing else will. When we are resenting the evil deeds of another we are not serving Love. The first commandment in the Bible is to love the Lord thy God with all thy heart and with all thy mind and with all thy strength, and love thy neighbor as thyself. God is Love. When we love God we are loving Love. And when we love God in another we are loving the Love in another. Love is the power of life: the wisdom of life: the joy of life living in and through us. When we hate we shut ourselves off from our good and cause others to shut themselves off from us. We find that hate causes us to have a barrier around us. The higher this wall of hate becomes the more insurmountable it seems.

The reason that Jesus was so effective as a teacher and a healer was because he based everything that he did on Love. He said, *Judge not that ye be not judged, for with what judgment ye judge, ye shall be judged, and with what measure ye mete, it shall be measured to you again.*[5] We judge others and then have to forgive our own judgments. Righteous judgment means to look through the appearances, to look through the apparent evil, to look through

[5] Matthew 7:1, 2.

the hate, and to recognize that each and every person is centered in Love. The next step is to know that Love is there and begin to call it forth. Just as water poured into a pump will act as a primer to cause more water to come forth, love poured into a situation will act as a primer to cause love to come forth. Look at the person who seems hard to love and silently affirm: "The love in me salutes the love in you." It is fruitless to think that we can overcome hate with hate. Hate will call forth a response in hate unless the chain of hate is broken by love. If we persist with love, it will overcome hate.

## Forgiveness Works

A man came to see me who was having difficulty with certain people in his office. He was tempted to fire them all, but he decided to try something different. So he forgave them over and over, each time substituting love for the resentment and appearances of hate. Eventually, when he was able to prove love to them through his actions the whole situation clarified. These people became trusted, loyal, and loving employees who appreciated him. I like to think of forgiveness as the giving up of all resentment, of all feelings of hostility, all feelings against another; substituting for them love and blessing. Forgiveness is not a matter of weakness, but of strength. It takes a strong man to be willing to say, "Irrespective of what you have done to me or to someone I love, I forgive you."

## *There Is No End to Forgiveness*

How often should we forgive? When Peter asked Jesus this question as to whether Peter should forgive seven times, Jesus replied that it should be *seventy times seven*. By this, Jesus meant that there is no end to our forgiving. We have to open the door for the other person to walk in. We may have to do this many times. Yet, we do not condone the wrong when we recognize the truth of being. In other words, we love the sinner but we do not have to love the sin.

### RELEASING OTHERS I AM RELEASED

Turning from the problems and cares of the day, I now consciously accept the Truth about God and myself. I know that God is the only Power and the only Presence. I know that I am the expression of God and that all the Father hath is mine. I am a divine, perfect, spiritual being, forever one with my Source. Turning from problems, I listen in the Silence for God's perfect answers. Turning from confusion, I accept the Peace that passeth all understanding. I let the perfect Life of God live through me.

I now release all those who have ever hurt or offended me. I forgive them completely. I forgive myself for the mistakes of the past. Releasing others, I am released. Love is the answer to my every need.

All that I need or desire is right within me. In this moment of Silence the work is done. The Spirit within me is the Substance of all my desires. I joyously and thankfully accept the good I desire for myself and the good I desire for others. That which I realize in the invisible becomes manifest in my world. Forgiveness has opened the door to divine right action in my world.

And so it is.

# ELEVEN

## Healing the Physical Body

*Much of your pain is self-chosen.*[1]
—Kahlil Gibran

The body is the instrument through which Spirit lives on earth. You Bible students would do well to look up all of the references to the body in the Bible. Paul called the body the temple of the living God. Jesus said: *Destroy this temple, and in three days I will raise it up.*[2] The people who heard him thought that he spoke of Solomon's Temple but he meant the temple of the body.

This body was meant to be a blessing, not a curse. The great plan of the Creator was that our bodies at all times be a joy and a comfort; that they be healthy from the day we come into this world until the day we go out of it.

### It Is a Sin to Be Unhealthy

I mean it. It is truly a sin to be sick and unhealthy. The word *sin* means *missing the mark, making a mistake.*

[1] Kahlil Gibran, *The Prophet* (New York: Alfred A. Knopf, 1958).
[2] John 2:19.

It is a mistake to think that it is natural or normal to be ill. Sin is a sense of separation from God, divine Good. As has been said, *there is only one sickness, a sense of separation from God.*

The early Hebrews believed that God was the Source of health. Health of body is promised in the inspired writings of scripture as the inevitable result of serving God with mind and heart.

*And thou shalt love the Lord thy God with all thine heart, and with all thy soul, and with all thy might. . . . And the Lord will take away from thee all sickness.*

Deuteronomy 6:5; 7:15

Sickness, by the Hebrews, was considered a punishment for sin and thus the evidence of soul sickness.

*Fools, because of their transgression, and because of their iniquities, are afflicted.* Psalms 107:17

There are many references in the Old Testament to the fact that sickness is the inevitable result of leaving the spiritual path. The Jews must have considered sickness an abomination before the sight of the Lord, for they required that those suffering from certain diseases be thoroughly cleansed and show themselves to the priests when they had recovered before they were allowed to approach the congregation. This was not just in the case of leprosy or other contagious diseases, but where there was an issue of blood or a skin affliction. The inference being that sickness was a matter of being contaminated.

There seems to be no thought of the worship of suffering which was the invention of the early Christians. This has persisted as a morbid element in Christianity. The idea that it is somehow virtuous to suffer; that the soul might be saved through the persecution of the body; that, since Jesus suffered on the cross, it was even walking in his footsteps to endure physical suffering; and, of course, the saddest thought of all—that sickness and pain are the *will of God* and therefore to be endured patiently until the Lord sees fit to remove them. This is the greatest fallacy of them all. For how can a person receive a healing if he believes in his heart that his sickness is the will of God?

Bodily trouble always comes from some form of ignorance, some form of *sin*,—not necessarily moral sin, or the saints would have been conspicuously healthy, but scientific sin, mistaken thinking. And this may come to us from our ancestors as an inherited disease in which we appear to have had no hand. If we look upon this as a *burden* laid upon us by a God whom we try to love, we shall think it our duty to bear it as long as our Deity pleases. This is resignation—a form of disease in itself, since it is generally due to mental inertia. The natural alternative to resignation is resentment at what seems to be an injustice.[3]

I believe that health, wholeness of mind and body, are man's divine inheritance, that had we continued to live as the Creator intended, eating of fresh fruits, vegetables, and grains provided, getting our exercise by tilling the soil, we would never know sickness. *God made man upright,* but we have certainly sought out many inventions, among them the myriad diseases of mind and body with which we occupy our time and thought today.

Before we can accept the healing we are seeking we

3 Adela Curtis, *The Way of Silence* (London: School of Silence, n.d.).

must rid ourselves of some of the fallacies of human thinking which bind our illnesses to us. Let's take a look at some of these fallacies.

## Fifteen Fallacies Concerning Sickness and Health

1. Sickness is the will of God and nothing can be done about it.
2. Disease is some kind of demon lurking on every side waiting to pounce upon us; that it can strike at any time.
3. Disease comes from a "bug" that is making the rounds and there is nothing we can do to escape it.
4. Ill health is inherited and therefore some people are doomed.
5. A person must continually compromise between health and sickness so that the best he can expect is some degree of good health.
6. Health is just a matter of luck; the unlucky ones get sick.
7. It is virtuous to suffer and "the good die young."
8. We have a perfect right to indulge in personal rage, resentment, fear or anxiety, all of which have no connection with our health.
9. Continuing good health is just too good to be true; a person can only expect health for a little while, and then some sort of a sick spell is inevitable.
10. The doctor keeps us healthy and good health depends upon having a good doctor; one can take any liberties in breaking the rules of health if he has a good doctor.

11. Good health depends upon taking drugs; the more drugs one takes the better his health.

12. Sickness has its advantages; it is a good way to get a little extra love and attention from the family.

13. As the years pile up we can expect less and less from our bodies; therefore a certain amount of ill health is to be expected as we get on in years.

14. We have to be continually working on the body to make it perform properly, dosing and doctoring it to make it run.

15. The body is a sinful thing that can only be redeemed through suffering. (This old puritanical idea comes from the belief that whatever gives pleasure is necessarily sinful. Since pleasure comes to us through the senses, the body was thought to be sinful, something to be renounced.)

## What Kind of Image Are We Setting Up for Ourselves?

I remember one time the late Don Blanding, who wrote *Joy Is an Inside Job*,[4] came to see us. I had never seen him looking so well. There was a new vitality about the man. He had just come from the mountains and while there had lost fifty or more pounds. He said that one day as he was starting out on a hike someone took his picture and he realized that he had let himself become a "great big fat man." He said he felt just like a hippopotamus limping along the road. Right then he decided to change his self-image, and he did. He set into mind a new image,

4 Don Blanding, *Joy Is an Inside Job* (New York: Dodd, Mead & Co., 1953).

one of being alive, strong, and vibrant. Something happened. He did not have to struggle to lose pounds, but soon he found that he was refusing the sort of food that had contributed to the old passé image. Gradually the outer began to conform to the inner and when I saw him he was a new man who radiated good health. He was now letting Life shine forth according to its true nature.

The idea of the perfect, divine image—Socrates *Divine Prototype*—within is not new. We don't have to make a face be a face, or a hand be a hand. We do not need to know how to function our various organs but divine Intelligence within us knows how to function the body according to the divine prototype, that perfect pattern within each one of us.

Judge Thomas Troward said in one of his lectures that we should conceive of a spiritual prototype for everything which becomes the root of the corresponding existence. He said:

The simplest practical method of gaining the habit of thinking in this manner is to conceive the existence in the spiritual world of a spiritual prototype of every existing thing, which becomes the root of the corresponding external existence. If we thus habituate ourselves to look on the spiritual prototype as the essential being of the thing, and the material form as the growth of this prototype into outward expression, then we shall see that the initial step to the production of any external fact must be the creation of its spiritual prototype. This prototype, being purely spiritual, can only be formed by the operation of *thought,* and in order to have substance on the spiritual plane it *must* be thought of as actually existing there. This conception has been elaborated by Plato in his doctrine of archetypal ideas, and by Swedenborg in his doctrine of correspondences; and a still greater teacher has said, "All things whatsoever ye pray and ask for, believe that ye *have* received them, and ye *shall* receive them." [5]

What Judge Troward is saying here is that we must create in our minds the ideal image and let it rest there with the belief that this ideal image will reproduce itself into outer manifestation as our perfect health. Then, we will be led each step of the way into paths of right action that we may live in accord with this divine image.

Don't you see that when we bow to the fallacies we let the image be established according to the fallacy, and thus we set up for ourselves a false image as being subject to disease, as being weak and tired and aging? As one of our friends wrote, it was such a great revelation to her that she didn't have to abide by the rule, "You can't expect to get entirely well at your age." Once she had altered that image the answers came and she stepped into an entirely new manifestation of health and well being.

### Age Has No Power Over Us But the Power We Give It

The fountain of youth within us knows nothing about age. Youth is a state of mind. It can go with us until the day we choose to leave this experience. I know people at ninety who are younger mentally and physically than others at forty. Right within us is the Source of our health. As we develop a consciousness of health as our divine birthright, this state will manifest in our experience.

It came out in one of our discussions at a recent seminar that sickness is bad data in our mental computer. We should red-flag the bad data and correct it. How are we

[5] Thomas Troward, *The Edinburgh Lectures on Mental Science* (New York: Dodd, Mead & Co., 1953).

going to overcome it? By loving God right within us, by loving Life within us. Perfect Love casts out fear and all of the children of fear. All of the mental equivalents which psychosomatic medicine sets up as causes of disease in the human body are actually children of fear stemming out of some hidden fear, and every one of them can be overcome by Love. This is what the commandment of Moses means. When we love the Law of divine Life right within us we are setting up a new equation in the computer of the subconscious mind and we will get new revised information out of the computer. *Garbage in—garbage out* is the way they say it in the data processing field. That which we put into the mind comes forth as our experience. Let's start today to set up the kind of mental image we really want to see emerge into manifestation. Resist the temptation to be sick in order to get love and attention; there are better ways. Beware of falling into the trap of old age. You need never be old and sick; it is not the law of your life.

Let us live in the Spirit, letting the Spirit live through us as our health and our life. As we let ourselves be completely in harmony with the Soul of the Universe nothing can attack us from without. *Know ye not that ye are the temple of God and that the spirit of God dwelleth in you?"* [6] Right within you is God's perfect health ready and willing to express in and through you—yes, eager to live Itself out into expression as you. Divine Intelligence right within you knows how to direct you to live in accord with the laws of life. The Wisdom within will teach you to make right decisions regarding the self. The very Source

[6] I Corinthians 3:16.

of Life within you will supply your vitality. The Power is continually available.

## Being Handicapped Need Not Be Unhealthy

It was once my privilege to meet and talk with a man who had no arms and hands. He showed me how he had learned to type with his toes and how he was able to cradle a telephone with his feet. He was able to produce exceptionally good oil paintings with his toes. As he demonstrated his abilities to me, he remarked: "I may be handicapped, but I'm no cripple." His remark stayed with me. This man packed more living into twenty-four hours than most of us who have all of our limbs intact.

Frances Brown was for several years my personal secretary. She is an amputee. As a child she had had infantile paralysis which caused her legs to remain undeveloped. Finally she was advised by her doctor when a young woman, to have one leg removed. The remaining leg seemed to have little usefulness and her doctor told her that she would never be able to walk. Frances fooled him. She learned to walk with crutches, using that "useless" leg so adroitly to balance herself that she became, not only mobile, but able to move about with considerable grace. Her hands and arms compensated by becoming stronger and stronger and today she literally floats about with the grace of a ballet dancer. She told me that her doctor was amazed at her agility and told her that she was just like a bumblebee. The bumblebee is not supposed to be able to fly—scientifically, that is. Its wingspread is not great enough to support its weight in the air. Yet, the bumblebee *does* fly. Scientifically, Frances was not supposed to be able to walk, yet, she *does* walk with the aid of crutches.

Another breakthrough came when she learned to drive her own car with the aid of hand controls. She is today one of the best drivers I have ever known. In fact, she lives such a normal life that no one ever thinks of her as handicapped. She believed that she could accomplish just about anything and so she did, including typing beautiful manuscripts for my books.

The handicapped person does not need to feel sorry for himself. Many of the letters which I receive are written on attractive notepaper bearing the sketches of Ann Adams of Jacksonville, Florida. Ann Adams is a most successful artist which would not be unusual except that Ann is paralyzed from the neck down. For four hours each day she is able to be out of her iron lung. During those four hours she does her drawings by holding a pencil in her mouth. Today her art work is seen everywhere on cards, stationery, and notepaper. When interviewed by a newspaper reporter, she said: "Don't make this a sad story. From time to time I may have the frustration of being helpless, but I'm essentially a happy person and a very grateful one." Ann Adams has won a place of distinction for herself in this world and, more than that, she is an inspiration to all who know her. She may be handicapped, but to me, she is not a cripple. She is another case of how the Intelligence of Life is able to compensate. If we use this Intelligence to the fullest Life will flow in and make up for any lack.

## Beware of Condemning the Body

Self-condemnation of the body is one of the most prevalent causes of ill health today. It is so easy to slip into habits of self-condemnation: *My eyes are getting worse and worse—my hearing is bad—I've got a bum ticker—my knees are stiff—my arthritis, etcetra, etcetra, etcetra.* Surrender up these old habit patterns and accept instead the divine prototype of a healthy body. Maybe we will be guided into ways and means to live a healthier life, but first, our thinking must change, and the rest will come easily. The Wisdom within us knows what is right for us.

Earlier in this book we spoke of the power of prayer on plants. We mentioned how Jesus illustrated this by cursing the fig tree. The body is just like a plant. It responds to blessing and cursing. If you bless the body and see it as the instrument of Spirit it will bless you. If you curse the body, and that is what we do when we condemn it by claiming ill health for ourselves, it does literally begin to wither and die like the fig tree in the Bible story.

If you think that the body is an evil thing, a gross or sinful thing that must be denigrated as a means of making its owner more spiritual, you are condemning the body and instead of making yourself more spiritual, you will suffer so many ills of the body that you won't have time to think of spiritual things.

The best way to get along with this body instrument is to bless it and release it and be so busy living the good life that you don't have time to dwell on the body. This does not mean that we are not to use good body hygiene, eat proper food, and exercise. As long as we live on this earth we should treat the body well, but I find that if we ask for guidance along these lines we are told what to eat, what to wear, and are inspired to exercise and do all of the things that are good for us without having to do them as a grim sort of punishment.

You are made of the Essence of Life, the divine Substance which can never become sick or decay, never become tired or worn out. It is eternal Substance that never runs out, never becomes depleted, old, or infirm. God in you knows nothing about age or sickness. God is forever young and so are you. Right this moment you are beginning again with a new vital image of Life expressing as wholeness and perfection. Bless each part of your body. It is God Life. Bless this life that you are living to the glory of God. Arise, take up your bed and walk—for you are free!

## Being Is a Verb

The word "being" is a verb. You are a divine, perfect spiritual *being*. You are Spirit *being* Its expression here on this earth. Emerson wrote: "Every spirit builds itself a house." Paul said: There are celestial bodies and bodies terrestrial.[7] You have been given this body instrument through which to live to the glory of God. Appreciate it for what it is, a most magnificent creation of Spirit. Every birth is a miracle. It has to be a manifestation of Spirit. It is too wonderfully planned to be anything else. I believe that we will always have some sort of a body instrument through which to express throughout eternity. We had

7 I Corinthians 15:40.

better start now to appreciate our body instrument and let it be healthy as it was intended to be.

## The Woman Who Learned How to Bless Her Body

Once a woman came to see us for a healing. She had three kinds of so-called incurable diseases. She had a heart condition that the doctors said she would have to learn to live with. She had diabetes and some other incurable (to medical belief) malady. She was miserable and frightened. We had a prayer treatment together such as we discussed in chapter four, and when we had finished she looked like a new person. She believed that she could be healed and she was healed. We gave her a meditation to take home with her that she might continue to keep her consciousness high. I am going to give it to you at the end of this chapter. It is titled, "I Bless My Body." I would like to remind you: the body should be a means of Grace. It is the Grace of God in your life, the illimitable love of God expressed in and through you. The divine You cannot be sick. Do not ever say "I am sick." The spiritual You is divine and perfect, made in the image and likeness of God. When you say, "I am sick, I am miserable, I have ill health," what you really mean is "my body is not functioning well." If your body is not functioning well it is because you are not thinking right. Yes, *God hath made man upright; but they have sought out many inventions.*[8] Get your thinking sorted out through spiritual mind treatment and you won't have any trouble with your body. You were not meant to be ill. Don't take it for granted that this is a nor-

8 Ecclesiastes 7:29.

mal way of life. It is thoroughly abnormal. You don't need to be unhealthy one minute longer. Turn over a new leaf today. Only your thinking is sick. Rise up into a new level of consciousness and your body will manifest this new mental pattern for it. Start out by blessing your body. This treatment I am about to give you has changed the lives of many people. Work with it faithfully and it will change you.

### I BLESS MY BODY

> *Know ye not that ye are the temple of God, and that the Spirit of God dwelleth in you?*

I bless my body.

It is the temple of God:—pure Spiritual Substance.

Every cell of my body is activated by Divine Intelligence.

Every organ in my body is regulated by the Involuntary Life within me, in perfect harmonious action.

Each organ in my body is a perfect part of a Perfect Whole—the Perfect Wholeness that is God expressing as me.

I bless my body and give thanks for it. It is a faithful servant provided and maintained to house the individualization of God known as myself.

I bless my body and release it in perfect confidence to the Father within who *neither slumbers nor sleeps* in His care for me.

I trust the Father within to beat my heart, digest my food, circulate my blood and harmonize the entire action of my body.

I am the temple of God.

The spirit of God dwells within me.

I thank Thee, Father, for Thy loving care.

                                        **And so it is.**

# TWELVE

## The Will to Live

*We die only when we are ready to die. We die when we want to die. We die because unconsciously we want to die, although rationally we may profess that we have everything to live for.*

*If we truly wish to live, if we have the incentive to live, if we have something to live for—then no matter how sick we may be, no matter how close to death, we do not die. We live, because we want to live.*[1]*—A. A. Hutschnecker*

A woman in England was dying of cancer. A relative visited her bedside and felt compelled to ask her, "What is it that you have always wanted to do more than anything in the whole world?"

The sick woman raised herself up on her elbow. A light came into her eyes that for a moment seemed to transform her into a radiant, alive being. At that moment she looked like her old vital self. She answered eagerly, "I've always wanted to go to Italy to study art, to visit the museums and galleries there."

1 Arnold A. Hutschnecker, *The Will to Live* (New York: Thomas Y. Crowell Co., 1951).

167

"That's easy," her aunt smiled, "I'll finance the trip if you'll go."

To the amazement of her family and everyone who knew her the patient began to get well. The change was immediately apparent. She did go to Italy to study art and a year later when her aunt visited her in Florence there was no trace of the former condition.

### The Will To Die

Betty L. had an obsession. She was the widow of a doctor and knew many doctors. So great was her interest in medicine that she worked whenever possible as a volunteer in doctors' offices. She could always be counted on to bring to any gathering the latest and goriest details of some terminal case, usually cancer. We sometimes wondered if she didn't spend most of her time thinking about cancer. Again and again she was heard to say that if ever she should have such a diagnosis she wanted the doctors to be absolutely honest. She wanted to know the truth. To her, cancer stood for that horrible death she had been dramatizing for so long. Another statement she made frequently was that if ever they did find that she had cancer she did not want to linger, she wanted to die at once.

One time when I was scheduled to lecture in La Jolla I heard that Betty was in the Scripps Clinic for observation. On the way to the lecture I stopped in to see her. There was a nurse in the room making some tests and she asked me to stop by after the lecture. I remarked to my wife, as we left, how well Betty looked—she was fairly beaming as if she was enjoying the situation thoroughly.

After the lecture we went back as promised and went directly to the room. Imagine our surprise to find the room vacant, the bed stripped, the flowers removed.

I quickly found a nurse and asked where to find Betty. The nurse said, "Didn't you know? She passed on about an hour ago. Her doctor came in to read her the report of the clinical tests. He told her that she had cancer. Within five minutes she was gone."

I knew the doctor very well and so I called him to ask about it. He told me that she did not have a terminal case, that he considered the cancer to be operable. His remark to me was, "Fear killed that woman."

### Giving the Order to Life

My wife's uncle died at ninety. He had never been sick a day in his life. He had never retired, never stopped working. He was a harness maker and every day he walked two miles to work and two miles back. His cheeks were rosy and his hair still black, his face unlined, his eyes bright. Why did he die at ninety? All his life he had said, "I'm going to live until I am ninety." He did. He had given the order to life. He had made it absolutely clear. At ninety he passed on. The choice had been made and life accommodated him.

### Choosing the Time

Can the will to live prolong our stay on earth? Does man choose the hour of his transition to the next experience? There are those who will answer "yes" to both questions.

Thomas A. Edison wrote in an article in one of the leading magazines of his day:

My grandfather ate carefully and lived to be one hundred and four years old. No disease killed him. He was perfectly well up to the time he died. He lost interest in life. The cells of which his body was composed were anxious to get away. So my grandfather told his children that he was going to his daughter's house to die. He went to her home, undressed, went to bed, and died. There was nothing the matter with him. He was simply tired of life. And my father died the same way.

### The Turning Point

"Do you know why people die?" This question was asked a friend of mine who was spending some time in a Los Angeles hospital. We'll call her Mary Jane, although that is not her real name. Mary Jane had been given two months to live. The doctors had suggested that she come in for some X-Ray treatments. No doubt she had given quite a little thought during her stay in the hospital to this business of dying.

And now the question was put to her point-blank by a little blue-eyed nun who had walked up to her and calmly asked her, "Do you know why people die?" Mary Jane had her own ideas but she said to the sister, "You tell me."

Those bright blue eyes seemed to get bluer as the sister gave her a searching look. Her answer was short and to the point. "Because they give up. You have work to do in this world." With that, she turned on her heel, walked out of the room and down the corridor as quietly as she had come.

Well, you can imagine how my friend felt. She had done a great deal of praying on this very subject. "Why, oh why, should I leave this life that I love so much. I'm not ready to go yet." And now, here was an answer, right out of the blue, so to speak, at least right out of those searching blue eyes. It was as if the Lord had sent his angel with an answer. Mary Jane lay very still and thought this one over.

## Man Never Heals Man

Mary Jane was not an average run-of-the-mill type of person. In certain circles she herself was considered to be a healer.

That is, when she prayed for other people they got well. Many had come to her for help. And now, here she was, in this crazy predicament unable to help herself. She had asked herself this question over and over, "Why can't I help myself?" And so she lay very still in her hospital bed, her pink cheeks just matching the beautiful pink roses that arrived fresh each day from her adoring husband. In the stillness of the room she waited for further illumination.

It came to her that she couldn't help herself because she was trying to do the work and man never heals man. Only the Spirit within can heal man. How had she helped others? She thought awhile. Well, certainly she did not believe that she, the human Mary Jane, did the healing. She had gone to the Father to whom nothing is impossible and she had been able, in perfect confidence, to release the problem to His ever-loving care. There was no flaw in her faith when the work was for another. But, with herself, she had felt that she had to give a good account of herself. *She* could not be sick. What would people think? Had there been a measure of spiritual pride holding her back? Furthermore, she now saw that she *had* given up. Underneath it all she had given up, because she couldn't see the answer. Here was her answer. Here was the key. She did have work to do and she wasn't giving up. From that moment on she started getting well. The healing took place in miraculous order, amazing the doctors and nurses and everyone who knew about it.

## Let's See What Happened Here

Mary Jane literally *took a new lease on life* as the saying goes. The Spirit within knows only Life, eternal Life.

When Mary Jane realized that she had work to do, that she had a purpose for living, she turned her attention away from death and became one with Life. Now she had the will to live, the will to continue. Like Job who received his healing when he prayed for his friends, Mary Jane turned away from her own problems and gave her entire attention to the good work she had done before in helping others. She began again to marvel at the wonder and the glory of God's perfect Life. Almost like flashbacks in a movie her mind began to play back the marvelous happenings she had witnessed in the lives of others. She saw again the woman who had rallied in what others had supposed to be her last hours here on earth. Color had come into that woman's cheeks and she had sat up in her hospital bed and praised God. The nurses had been astonished when she asked for food and said she wanted to get up and get dressed. The nurses had marveled but Mary Jane had glorified God in her heart. She remembered the baby who had been healed instantaneously before her very eyes; the man who had been healed of alcoholism; the couple who had found love for each other in what had seemed to be a hopeless marriage. She felt again the exhilaration of being at hand at these times, privileged to be a close observer of these mighty works. How wondrous are Thy works, O Lord! How could she have doubted? What God has done once He can do again and did He not promise that nothing should be impossible *if* we believed?

This was the beginning of Mary Jane's healing. It took place without her having to do anything about it. Once she had taken her attention away from her sick body and given it entirely over to God's work, the body began to reflect the change in her thinking. Soon the doctors released her. "Do you know why people die?" the little nun had asked her. People die because they mentally stop living. Life is to be lived. It's a matter of facing life and living it.

Various people come to mind who have recovered from serious illnesses, some of them with dramatic healings which completely baffled their doctors, only to pass on soon after from some entirely different cause. These were people who had expressed a desire to leave this life. It has been said, "Every death is a suicide," and I have come to believe that it is true.

## The Decision Is Personal

Never again will I attempt to mentally hold a person in this life. I learned this lesson many years ago when I was called to the bedside of a woman in a coma. Day after day I went to see her and silently prayed at her bedside. Since she was in this unconscious state I talked to her silently, assuring her that she was needed, that she belonged here with her family. Finally, one day she opened her eyes and spoke to me. To my great surprise she reproached me for having called her back to this life. She said that she had wanted to go on and join her husband who had already left this experience. To me this was an entirely new idea. I had not thought, prior to this time, that anyone asking for prayers might *choose* to die. This woman recovered from her illness but shortly afterward passed on from an entirely different cause. After that experience I always pray that the person be released to perfect Life, whether it is here or hereafter.

Since then I have had numerous cases where the patient has slipped over to the other side several times before passing on. In every case the reports have been that once having glimpsed the new experience there was no desire to return. In fact, the descriptions of this *other-world experience* have been so ecstatic that one could hardly wish to detain them here.

## Death Is Not Defeat

Do not feel that you have failed if you have prayed long and faithfully and still the one for whom you prayed passes on. The innermost desire of the one for whom you prayed will prevail. It is his choice. You have no right to make it for him according to human judgment. Both my wife and I have come to feel that death is never defeat, that it is often a freeing up, a promotion, one might say. Surely, we have had many proofs that death is not the end of living. Often it is the choice of the person involved. Just as one becomes tired of elementary school and longs to go on to high school; just as one becomes tired of a vacation and is eager to return home, so do we mortals actually long to return to our heavenly home. Who knows what heavenly voices are heard, what beautiful music beckons us on at last to that new and glorious experience. We have seen the faces of those about to make the transition glow with unspeakable joy; we have seen them pass over with expressions transformed, their faces alight. Many who hovered on the threshold of life have reported that they were met by loved ones who were eager to welcome them there. During the interim of glimpsing the new realm, they say that they are aware of the Love of God as they had never before experienced it. If this is true, who could urge them to stay? Who would selfishly hold such a one in this earthly experience? I would rather believe that we choose to be born and we choose to die and *The Lord shall preserve thy going out and thy coming in from this time forth, and even for evermore.*[2]

In my clipping file is a story that appeared in the *San Diego Union* a few years ago. It tells about a woman in New Orleans who had been in the psychiatrist's office

2 Psalms 121:8.

approximately ten minutes discussing her problems when she fell dead.

She had been suffering from asthma but that wasn't what killed her. An autopsy showed she had been in fairly good physical health. She had taken no poisonous drug. She had neither shot nor stabbed herself. In fact, there wasn't a bruise on her.

In the absence of the slightest medical cause, doctors decided Mrs. J. had killed herself solely through her own will. She had wished herself to death.

A Navy psychiatrist cites this example of the death of Mrs. J. in discussing the strange phenomenon of persons committing suicide by literally wishing for death. He comments: "There are many unexplained medical deaths which are actually due to suicide through the psychological method. I have known many cases in which a patient actually committed suicide without external violence."

## The Will to Live

A good book on this subject is *The Will to Live* by Arnold A. Hutschnecker. In this book Dr. Hutschnecker, an outstanding phychiatrist shows how you can avoid illness by understanding the emotional upsets that produce them. How often you hear a person say of his boss or colleague, "He makes me sick," or "She gives me a pain." The speaker would be astonished to learn that he has uttered a little-known scientific truth. He is probably only conscious of a headache. He doubtless does not realize that physical pain—even illness—is the body's response to emotion.

In defining illness, Dr. Hutschnecker says:

For more than a generation now, great physicians have been preaching that man is not a machine put together on an assembly line, but one complex and mysterious whole. Slowly we are relearning the ancient truth that if a part is ill, the *whole* is ill.[3]

In this interesting book the author cites case after case which demonstrate the emotional pathways that lead to physical illness. He writes:

We have the power; that positive force within us, the will to live. This is the powerful ally of those whose profound wish is to be well. In response to their rational, conscious effort, the will to live rises to their aid in a thousand big and little ways.[4]

## Man Is a Triune Being

I have known hundreds of different people who seemed dead set on destroying themselves. Some of them succeeded; others were able to find a reason for living, a new philosophy of being which not only changed their mental approach to this business of living but was the means of changing their physical bodies to the extent that they recovered from the chronic illnesses that they had brought upon themselves and became whole in spirit, mind, and body. I cannot over emphasize this. Every healing is first a healing of the inner self. Man is a triune being. He is spirit, mind, and body.

[3] Hutschnecker, *The Will to Live.*          [4] Ibid.

### THE WILL OF GOD IN ME IS LIFE

The Will of God in me is Life not death. All destructive thoughts, despair, discouragement, belief in sickness, lack and limitation, are thoughts of death and I refuse to give them place in my consciousness. I turn my face resolutely to the life-giving Power of God which is everlasting Life and claim this Life for myself. Matter has no power of itself to become sick or diseased. *Matter is Spirit in ever-changing form.* Spirit uses matter as an instrument of expression, but is not confined or limited by this instrument. God is the One Source of Life. This Life is my life now. Yes, *in my flesh shall I see God,* as I let Life live through me unimpeded by human concepts of human limitation. The Will of God in me is Life and this Life only will I serve.

And so it is.

# THIRTEEN

## Some Notable Healings and What We Can Learn from Them

*And these signs shall follow them that believe; In my name shall they cast out devils; they shall speak with new tongues; they shall take up serpents; . . . and if they drink any deadly thing, it shall not hurt them; they shall lay hands on the sick, and they shall recover.*—Mark 16:17,18

There are signs following for them who believe. This is not something new and peculiar to just a few. There have been healings down through the years. Every time perfect Love casts out fear another devil has been cast out. People who believe not only do speak in new tongues but learn to keep their conversation "in heaven" and thereby speak with new understanding. They have been able to deny the power of poison so that it does not hurt them, and all those whom they touch spiritually, mentally, and physically are healed.

In this chapter I am going to share with you some notable healings that stand out in my mind.

### A Medical Doctor Turns to Spiritual Healing

The late Dr. Rebecca Beard had been a practicing medical doctor for twenty years when she discovered spiritual mind healing. There came a time in her life when the love of scientific knowledge did not seem to answer her need. She was told by her colleagues in the medical profession that she must put her affairs in order for she could not live through another heart attack. It was then that Dr. Beard surrendered her life completely to God, and the Power became real to her as a part of her very being. She prayed: "If it is possible, take this from me. Either take it from me or take me. I have gone as far as I can."

With this act of surrender came a great spiritual illumination. She knew then that she was healed and that the rest of her life would be given to helping others find that kind of healing.

In her book *Everyman's Search* [1] she tells of one of these healings. She had prayed for a sign, a healing that would convince her, with her medical background, and prove to the world that anything could be healed spiritually.

In reporting this healing, Dr. Beard admitted that cancer was, to her, the great hurdle. Her thought was that possibly everything could be accomplished through prayer but this. Yet, something deep within her kept telling her that she dared not step out into the world of spiritual healing unless she was absolutely sure that there was no such barrier that could not be overcome through God's healing power.

[1] Rebecca Beard, *Everyman's Search* (New York: Harper & Row, 1950).

As a medical doctor she had seen so many people suffering from cancer that this, to her, was a tremendous hurdle to pass. And so she prayed, "Father, show us a condition that is unquestioned, about which no one can rationalize. We want to see something that is so evident in its outward manifestation that everyone can see it. We want to see something that is called incurable. We want to see an instantaneous healing, and we want to see it complete and made possible without any agency but prayer."

Several weeks later her opportunity came. A friend, Alice Newton, came from Leavenworth, Kansas, to see the Beards. She had known Dr. Beard when she practised in that city. Dr. Beard was shocked at her appearance; her abdomen was larger than a woman at full-term pregnancy, her emaciated body scarcely able to carry such a burden. She asked Dr. Beard, "Do you think that I can be healed with prayer and nothing else?"

At that point Dr. Beard thought, "This is it!" She'd asked for it and now she had what she prayed for and it gave her a sinking feeling. She wrote:

> You see, I did believe with my conscious mind, but my subconscious said, "Help Thou mine unbelief." Then I heard myself saying, "Yes, Alice, I believe. But I want to see it. I need to see it." [2]

Alice agreed to go home and map out a program and a schedule, to follow it every day, and to have absolute faith that their prayers would be answered and that the Lord would heal her. She did just that. She went home, canceled all social obligations, doing only simple things about the house. She rested, walked in the open air,

[2] Ibid.

read her Bible, sang hymns, and prayed. She confidently awaited her healing and Dr. Beard says that in none of her letters did she ever suggest failure. And, of course, this greatly strengthened the faith of the Beards who were praying for her.

The medical doctor in Leavenworth, who visited Alice often, was a friend of theirs. For two years Alice kept the faith and often encouraged the doctor for she had a spiritual conviction. Finally, one night, the miracle happened.

That night Alice retired shortly after her husband left for his work as a warder at the Leavenworth prison. He worked from midnight until morning. She went to sleep as usual and as she slept she had a vision. She saw the disciples asleep as Jesus came down the mountainside from his lone vigil of prayer. His face was full of sorrow as he looked at the sleeping men, then he glanced over and smiled at her. Like a motion picture, the scene shifted and it was the day of the crucifixion. She saw the cross being lowered into the hole that had been made ready for it. The body of the master was already nailed upon it. In her dream she was torn by the thought of how the jar would hurt him and she cried out, "Oh, my Jesus," putting up her hand to steady his body and ease his suffering. It was at that moment that her hand dropped to her abdomen.

Turning on the light she saw that it was three o'clock. Only then she realized that her abdomen was perfectly flat. The huge accumulation was gone! Immediately she felt all around her for moisture, thinking surely something had passed, but the bed was dry. There was no pain. Her spirit rejoiced, and she knew something wonderful had happened. So she turned out the light and waited.

Her husband came home rather early that morning. He felt, somehow, that something had happened. His excitement was so great when he heard the news that, to relieve him, she asked him to go for her friend, the doctor, cautioning him not to tell. Alice was a woman with a marvelous sense of humour, so before the doctor came she slipped a pillow under the bedcovers. She wanted to hear him scold. As he came in and stood at the foot of her bed, he shook a warning finger, saying, "Alice, I told you to let me tap you." She only smiled at first, then she said, "Yes, Doctor, and I told you that God was going to take care of me. See what He has done," and she pulled the pillow out and dropped it to the floor.

The doctor was speechless for a moment, then he rushed around the bed and knelt at her side. His questions came short and fast in his excitement. "What passed?" "What came away?" "Was there water?" "Was there blood?" "Did you perspire heavily?" "What was it?" To all she answered truthfully, "Nothing." Finally his questions ceased, for her answers continued to be, "No, nothing passed—nothing came away." At last he said quietly, "No one but God could perform a miracle like that."

She stayed in bed for a week because they thought it was wise. People passed through the house constantly to see her in the days that followed. At the end of the week she was weighed, and it was found that she had lost thirty-eight and a half pounds! That had disappeared overnight. And that was the answer to our prayer. That was a condition which no one could say had not existed. It could not be rationalized away. It was an instantaneous healing. No one could explain it. Where did thirty-eight and a half pounds of actual weight go in three hours? That was the miracle. I had wanted to see something which I could not explain. God had answered my prayer.

Later, Alice came to St. Louis and asked if I wished to

examine her. This I did, and found every organ fresh and virginal as though she had never been ill. She lives today. This happening has had a strange sequel. During the past twelve years the Leavenworth newspaper and the *Kansas City Star* have mentioned this remarkable recovery each January on the anniversary of Alice's healing! [3]

## What We Can Learn From This Healing

Here we have recognition, realization, and release. The recognition that the Almighty Power could heal Alice, combined with the realization that it could happen to her. The criticalness of her situation forced her to abandon herself completely to the Power. But the thing that this story drives home is the single-minded, nonwavering persistence showed by Alice and Dr. Beard. It did not happen overnight as most of us demand that healings should happen. It took two years of persistent prayer and fasting from negative thinking. Along the way, there must have been many occasions when Alice was tempted to sink back into the world's belief about her condition. But she persisted and the healing came. Dr. Rebecca Beard wanted to see a miracle, one that she could not explain and God answered her prayer.

## It Couldn't Happen—But It Did

One of the most dramatic healings I have ever heard was told by Louise Eggleston of Richmond, Virginia. My wife and I went to hear her lecture at the First Methodist Church in San Diego in 1956. How glad we were that we

[3] Ibid.

had gone! It was a memorable experience. Mrs. Eggleston had a serenity that was centered in Love. You felt her great conviction. In the course of her talk she told of how a young couple had come to her some years before asking her to pray that they have a child. The medical doctors had told them that this was impossible.

Scientifically, it couldn't happen, but it did. The young woman became pregnant and the child was born, a little girl. Imagine their joy! However, their happiness was short lived because they soon discovered that the baby was not right. It had, as I remember, no proper bone structure, the bones were soft and continued to disintegrate so that the baby grew progressively worse. Since this child had been a gift of God, truly a miracle, the parents, Louise Eggleston, and the minister of the church all felt that God would heal her. They all prayed without ceasing for the little girl and still she grew worse. Finally, when it looked as if the baby just couldn't live, someone suggested that they put her on the altar just as Abraham had been willing to sacrifice Isaac, and give her to God. To the young couple who had wanted a baby so much, this was truly an act of faith. It was complete surrender of all their hopes and desires. So that this symbolic act would have greater meaning they gathered at the church and actually placed the child on the altar and joined in releasing her to her heavenly Father. It was then that the miracle took place. From that moment on the baby improved. Mrs. Eggleston reported that the last person she talked to before leaving Richmond to come to the West Coast was this little girl, now a healthy, active nine-year-old, perfect in every way.

## What We Can Learn From This Healing

The dominant truth in this story is that we must judge by righteous judgment rather than human judgment. When human judgment seems so overpowering that it may even seem ridiculous to trust in God Power, then there must be total surrender to the Omnipotence. The act of faith of putting the child on the church altar may seem to many to be overdramatizing the principle of surrender, but at times it takes a dramatic step to cause us to release the situation to God. Man's extremity is truly God's opportunity.

## An Instantaneous Healing

One time a grandmother called me from another city. She said that their baby granddaughter was suffering from pneumonia. She seemed to be dying right in front of their eyes. "She's not breathing at all!" she sobbed into the telephone.

I realized that my part in this healing was not to get caught up in the appearances. The family was distraught, but I knew that the perfect Life of God in this child had never been touched by this apparent condition. I asked the grandmother to join with me in scientific prayer. I can't remember just how the prayer went, for it was spontaneous. I only know that I had a realization that this little girl was a divine, perfect, spiritual being; that perfect Life which cannot be contaminated by disease or germs for Life is eternal, changeless.

Almost at once the grandmother called me back. She

said that she had, as directed, seated by the crib, joined me in prayer. It couldn't have been more than a minute or two, she told me, when there was a sound from the crib, a little loose cough, and when she looked the child sat up in the crib and for the first time in days, breathed naturally. The color had come back into her face and her breathing was normal. What had happened? Where had the congestion, the mucus, the phlegm gone? They had disappeared. Not a single symptom of the condition remained. The little girl who had been passive and inert, so that at times the family thought that she was dead, was now alert and full of her normal enthusiasm, asking for breakfast, eager to play.

I do not wish to imply that I healed this child. I simply was privileged to witness it by long-distance telephone. Yes, somebody prayed and a healing took place, a rather dramatic one. We feel the hand of God at work here. When something like this happens one can only feel a deep sense of humility. To God belongs the glory. There is only one healing Power, the Power of God. As we recognize and unify with the Power the healing takes place as easily as when the light causes the darkness to vanish. At such a time the one who prays feels like a spectator who is privileged to watch the Great Power at work.

## Disease Has No Power of Its Own

I have not only witnessed instantaneous healings, I have experienced them. Have you ever seen anyone healed instantly? Have you ever had a blinding headache, or a bad sore throat with all of the symptoms of a cold coming on, and then the next moment have it completely disappear? When this happens to you or to someone around you, you begin to see that disease couldn't have had any power of its own. If there was power in disease, healing could never take place. Nor is it a matter of God Power fighting with the power of evil. Spiritual healing comes through an awareness that God is the only Power and the only Presence. The healing awaits our acceptance of this verity. Every healing would be an instantaneous healing if we could have an instantaneous acceptance of the mighty power of God working in and through us. As the late Dr. Harry Douglas Smith proclaimed, "It is only one thought away." [4]

## There Are Different Kinds of Healing

Generally, we think of healing as it refers to the physical body. There are many different kinds of healing. The effects of healing show in many areas of life. As we have said, there is only one sickness, a sense of separation from Life. A healing of this sense of separation results in fulfillment in various areas of living.

A man just called me from Tuscon, Arizona, with a good report. A month ago he had called telling me that he had been ill for quite some time, his business had just about gone to pieces, and there was much dissension in his home. This man had reached bottom. Judging by appearances it was a pretty gloomy picture.

Today he called to give me the good news. Right away

[4] Harry Douglas Smith, *The Secret of Instantaneous Healing* (West Nyack, N.Y.: Parker Publishing Co., Inc., 1965).

I could sense that he had been restored to wholeness of spirit, mind, and body. In the outer picture, he is now expressing good health, his business is prosperous, and his home life is harmonious again. So, you see, there was really one healing with many side effects. What happened? When he called the first time, I did not sympathize with him; neither did I advise him what to do to improve his health, his business, or his home life. I had a spiritual mind treatment with him over the telephone. As we joined in this scientific prayer, we affirmed the Truth that he was whole, perfect, and lacking in nothing; that he was immersed in God's Love. We prayed the Lord's Prayer together. There is nothing like the Lord's Prayer to reestablish a sense of unity with God where there has previously been a sense of separation. I asked him to agree with me that, irrespective of the appearances, he was now enjoying perfect health, a prosperous business, and harmony in his home. In other words, we erased from mind the negative picture that he had first presented to me.

I did not try to figure out in my mind what he should do to bring all this about. I had to trust the all-knowing Intelligence within him and all of life to bring these answers into his experience in a way that he could accept them. If I had tried to figure out what was right for him I would actually have been figuring out what was right for me. I can only see life, judge life, express life from my own point in consciousness. We all express life from our own state of awareness. Each one is different, no two are alike. How then could I judge for another what might be his highest good?

I would like to emphasize that what I did was to have

a spiritual mind treatment with this man. I did not pray, "O Lord, take away these terrible problems from this man." Nor did I pray that he be given the strength to bear them. Instead I turned away from the appearances and knew that he was from the beginning of time a divine, perfect spiritual being surrounded by God's Love. I knew that the appearances of disease, lack, and inharmony were not the Truth about him and that there was no power in them. Appearances are based upon human judgment. In treatment, we rely upon *righteous judgment*. Facts are not reliable. Truth transcends facts. Today, our friend in Tuscon, after telling me that his whole life had changed, remarked, "You are a terrific healer!"

"Wait a minute," I exclaimed. "I did not heal you. Jack Addington has never healed anybody. The Spirit of Truth within you has restored your wholeness and the effects of that wholeness are now apparent in your life and affairs."

## There Are Many Healings

In this book I have given you a few case histories of healings as they come to mind. In each instance I have permission to tell of the experience. I do want to emphasize that spiritual mind healings are much more common than most people realize. A healing is a very personal thing and many people are loathe to talk about them. I know of hundreds of healings that I would like to share but space make this impractical.

I confess we almost come to take them for granted. In most cases the healing comes so naturally that it no longer seems to be a miracle, but truly a law-abiding event.

Of the hundreds of letters I receive each week, a large number tell of demonstrations of God's healing power. Many of them are thrilling. People all over the world are having these demonstrations. This is the term commonly used to describe healings of physical conditions as well as healings of lack and inharmony of one sort and another. We call them demonstrations because they are just that— demonstrations of the divine Law in action. Demonstrations appear when man is able to recognize the unreality of negative thinking, emotional blocks, and belief in false appearances which have seemed to block the flow of divine Life through his body and affairs. When man is able, in one area of his life or another, to accept the Truth of Being, the Truth does set him free.

We might compare this action to a stream flowing down from the mountains. The water is clear and abundant, the source seems endless. The source does not hold back. The stream pours itself out freely, merrily flowing down the mountainside until it comes to a place where its channel is blocked with rocks and other debris. Then, the water begins to back up and, for a time, the stream seems to make little headway. Then, along comes someone who says, "This debris does not belong here. It is stopping the flow of water. This stream was meant to flow." The debris is removed and the stream continues to flow according to its nature. And so it is with the stream of Life, that wonderful River of Life, *the streams whereof make glad the city of God.*[5] The stream of Life is willing and, unless we dam it up with negative thinking, it will continue to pour Itself out to us as all that we need. Our part is to clean out the

5 Psalms 46:4.

debris; the River of Life will do the rest. We do this by cleaning out our negative thinking, cleansing our minds of fear and resentment, jealousy and resistance to situations and people. I think we all know areas in our thinking where we have damned up the flow of Good.

## Beware of False Gods

Anything that stands between us and our divine perfection is a false god. We must ask ourselves, "What false gods am I worshipping?" To what are we giving our attention? The word worship means *to assign great worth to.* What is it that we worship, assign great worth to? If we are giving our attention to some *enemy,* some erroneous situation in our lives such as ill health, poverty, or dissension, then we are letting it come between us and our Good. We are letting it become a false god to us.

God does not deny us our healing. It is we who block the flow of Good in our lives. *All that the Father hath is thine.* Our part is to accept our divine inheritance that we may be the children of God, sons and heirs to the Kingdom of God within.

### PERFECTION IS UNCHANGING

Perfection is unchanging. The perfection of God cannot be altered, depleted, or exhausted. Nothing can be taken away from it or added unto it. This perfection is constantly expressing through man, the perfect creation of God.

Christ, God Life, as man, is changeless perfection.

God is Life, a Life that is perfect, complete and whole, yesterday, today, and throughout eternity. This Life, in man, is not dependent upon outer conditions or circumstances. Nothing from without can injure or interfere with the perfection of God in and through man. There is no power in conditions. There is only Power in God.

Man is not subject to sickness and death. In Truth, he is eternal Life, a divine, perfect, spiritual being; completely uncontaminated by disease or death. This is the Truth. In It we rest, trusting and unafraid.

And so it is.

# FOURTEEN

## Keeping a Prayer Ledger

> *For verily I say unto you, that whosoever shall say unto this mountain, Be thou removed, and be thou cast into the sea; and shall not doubt in his heart, but shall believe that those things which he sayeth shall come to pass; he shall have whatsoever he sayeth.*—Mark 11:23

Had you thought encyclopedias were dull, dry reading? You thought wrong. What drama! What exciting life adventure is packed between the covers of each volume! Endless plots for novels and plays, such beauty, such pathos, so much inspiration is to be found in real life. If you question this, read the story of George Müller. Here was a man who possessed the mountain-moving kind of faith. He spoke his word and knew that it would not return void. Although he may never have heard of the term, he used the techniques of spiritual mind treatment described in this book.

George Müller was a preacher and philanthropist but his claim to fame is a prayer ledger that came out of his ninety-three years packed full of living. He entered in his ledger some twenty-seven thousand prayers. In a ledger, the right-hand page always balances with the left side and this ledger was no exception. All twenty-seven thousand prayers were answered and the answer recorded on the right. Did you doubt that prayers are answered? Perhaps your problem is that you do not go back and record the answers that come, relating them to the prayer that was responsible for them. George Müller was as methodical as a scientist in recording his prayers and their results.

We first hear of Müller when he became minister of a small congregation at Devonshire, England in the year 1830. Then only twenty-five years old, he was a man of faith as you shall see. He contended that the temporal as well as the spiritual needs of life could be met by prayer and so his first act was to abolish pew rents and refuse to take a fixed salary. After two years in his first parish, he moved to Bristol where he lived for the rest of his life devoting himself to the care of orphaned children. Even by today's standards, his orphanage was not a small operation. Remember, George Müller did not live in a welfare state with a liberal government handing out millions of dollars for public welfare. He depended entirely upon God's Love as expressed through voluntary giving. Starting out with a few orphans he soon increased their number to two thousand! They were housed in five very large houses erected for that purpose near Bristol. Imagine the needs of two thousand children! No wonder George recorded twenty-seven thousand prayers in his ledger!

According to Müller's faith, the money, the food, and all that was needed continued to come in through voluntary gifts. There were no radio programs then to espouse his cause, nor were there television programs to dramatize his needs, giving a telephone number for listeners to call in a pledge. About the only publicity his work received was a little narrative entitled *The Lord's Dealings with George Müller,* which he wrote. It received wide circulation and encouraged many to give to his work.

The story is told that one day the cooks came to him and told him that there was nothing in the houses to eat. The last bit of flour had been scraped from the bins, the last potato had been eaten. "We are going to have to put out the fires," they sadly announced, "for there is no more food to cook." How would you feel if two thousand hungry children depended on you for their breakfast? George Müller was not daunted. Remembering that thousands of his prayers had already been answered, he did not doubt that this prayer would also be answered. In his mind, he possibly pictured his prayer ledger and all of the carefully inscribed answers there as he told the cooks, "Don't put out the fires, the Lord will provide for us."

Later in the day a tremendous van pulled up in front of the houses. It was filled with provisions of every kind. *Before they call I will answer.* Even as George Müller prayed, someone had been led to meet the need. Another answer went into the prayer ledger. George Müller's faith was not in vain.

Does this event seem like a miracle to you? It certainly was answered prayer.

One time in 1956 I was browsing through a used bookstore in Victoria, British Columbia, when I came upon a large tome, about a thousand pages, giving an account of all of George Müller's prayers. We were traveling in a small foreign automobile and I felt I could not add another book to our luggage, but I have always regretted not acquiring this book. Someday I shall find it again.

It is interesting to note that the orphanages must have become so well established that they no longer needed Müller's supervision for when he was past seventy he started out on a preaching mission which lasted seventeen years and included India, Australia, and China, as well as Europe and America. Think of the faith this man was able to convey to his hearers! Consider the faith it took to get to all of these places in an age that did not have our methods of fast transportation. George Müller went on to his next glorious assignment in 1898 after a wonderfully fulfilled and happy life of walking with the Lord.

Would you like to start a prayer ledger? I will tell you how. Go to a stationery store and get yourself a copybook or, better yet, a hardbacked daily journal such as used for bookkeeping records. On the left page write your prayer. Do not dwell on the symptoms or the lack but on the need to be met. Make this a scientific prayer, a spiritual mind treatment. I am sure that George Müller's prayers were scientific prayers, spiritual mind treatments, else they would not all have been answered. A scientific prayer recognizes that Universal Mind Power, everywhere present, is able to do all things for us through us. It establishes in the mind of the one praying a consciousness of oneness with the Infinite. It accepts the need as already met, thus reversing the belief in lack or disease of the one praying. Because of this the prayer ends on a note of high expectancy by giving thanks for the manifestation as if it were already manifest. When you have established your prayer on this basis, release it with assurance. Should you start worrying again about your need, go back and read your prayer again and again until you can release the problem with perfect confidence. *Let patience have her perfect work, that ye may be perfect and entire, wanting nothing.*[1] Do not hurry your answer. It will come in the right and perfect time, in the right and perfect way. Do not outline how it shall be accomplished, but watch for your answer so that you will recognize it when it comes. Often we become so involved in delineating our next needs that we fail to realize that the last prayer has been answered. We actually forget that we ever prayed for that need. This is the value of a prayer ledger. It builds faith.

Do not be like the old couple who prayed for bread. Shortly afterward there was a knock at the door and there stood a man with two loaves of bread under his arm for them. Reluctantly the old man took the bread and, turning to his wife, said, "That's good, but I wish it had come from the Lord."

Your answer may come through man, but it is still the working of the Divine Law. Each prayer is answered in the way that the recipient can accept it and understand it. Your prayer may come in such a simple, commonplace way that you will take it as a matter of course not realizing that it is as much a miracle as if it came accompanied with ringing bells and flashing lights. The important thing is that you conclude the transaction by writing down the details of the answer on the right hand page facing your prayer. Give thanks and turn to a clean page so that you will be ready to write down a new prayer and a new answer. Keep your prayer ledger private to you unless you

1 James 1:4.

are sure that the other person shares your faith. Doubting Thomases are no help in accepting answered prayer. Be faithful with your prayer ledger. Who knows, perhaps you, too, will end up with twenty-seven thousand prayers answered. George Müller did.

Twenty years ago my wife and I worked out an abreviated version of the prayer ledger, one that can be carried in a person's pocket. So popular is this little book that it has been necessary to reprint it each year. It is called *Your Miracle Book*.[2] Thousands of people consider it just that. Someday I am going to write a sequel entitled, *The Miracles of the Miracle Book*. *Your Miracle Book* is simple to use but it is necessary to follow instructions to the letter exactly as they are given. It is an exercise in faith building that produces results. You must ask yourself, "What is it that I really want out of life?" If you want it enough to do something about it, then this book may be of real assistance to you. It can help you so much in causing wonderful things to happen in your life that you will agree that it is truly a *miracle* book.

In this adventure in spiritual living you start with thanksgiving. Pages eight, nine, ten, and eleven have been left blank. On them you are to write down every single thing you have to be thankful for. Sit quietly and let your mind explore every facet of your life to discover these items for thankfulness. Your talents, your skills, your friends, your family, your possessions, your health, your faith, your happiness, your understanding, all are things for which you can be thankful. List them all. Nothing is

---

2 *Your Miracle Book*, Abundant Living Foundation, Box 100, San Diego, California 92138, 50¢.

too trivial to give thanks for. This is the first step and the most important one. It is based on a law of Life. Unless you can give thanks—go no further.

Now, with a pencil and a piece of paper, sit down in a quiet place and think about the things you would like to have happen in your life. Maybe you want better health, a better job, more understanding with your family. Perhaps your heart's desire is for love and companionship. Do not hesitate or feel selfish or greedy in listing your desires. Put them all down on this sheet of paper. After you have written all of the things you can think of, go through the list and select the three that are the most important to you. In the order of their importance, write down these three desires on the first blank page in the back of the book. Ultimately you will add to this list but it is important at this stage to list three desires only.

As you go on you may find that you ask less and less for things and come to ask more for intangibles such as *an understanding heart,* but as long as you have need for *things* do not feel selfish or guilty about asking for them. God never judges or condemns us. Jesus said, *It is the Father's good pleasure to give you the kingdom,*[3] and assured us that if we ask the Father for bread he will not give us a stone.

Now, when you have both lists recorded in the book read them over every day, preferably at night before you go to sleep. Always start with the list in the front of the book. Mentally give thanks with all your heart for these blessings. This will firmly impress on your mind that your good comes from the One Source *without which was not*

3 Luke 12:32.

*anything made that was made.* This will build for you undreamed of faith. *Faith is the substance of things hoped for, the evidence of things not seen.*[4]

Now you are ready to turn to the back of the book and take a look at your first three desires. For each desire ask yourself the following questions.

1. Does it exist?
2. Does it exist for me?
3. Is it right for me?
4. Can I accept it?

When you have settled upon your three greatest desires and feel certain that they could exist for you, be right for you, and most important be accepted by you, release them mentally to the Creative Medium, the Universal Mind Power. Let go and let God!

As you read over your list of desires each day give thanks for the things that have not yet appeared as well as the things that are already in your experience. Mentally appropriate each thing or circumstance, feel as you would feel if you already had it, revel in it, *believe that ye receive them and ye shall have them.*

Prayer is turning away from man's lack and looking to God's Abundance. Expect your desires to come from God *in ways ye do not know.* Do not wonder how it can be done or through whom it will be done. God has ways we know not of and that is His business. All you need to do is take the human steps as they present themselves to you from time to time.

As the desires in the back of the book come into your

4 Hebrews 11:1.

experience—and they surely will—cross them off and put them in the front of the book and continue to give thanks for them. Replace them in the back with new desires.

Be careful not to become impatient. Like seeds, some desires take a little time to *come up*. Sometimes a year may go by but each seed is bound to produce fruit. My first book, *The Hidden Mystery of the Bible*, took twelve years to be realized but eventually it was made manifest exactly as I had visualized it.

You will soon realize that there is nothing in the world that you cannot have if you seek it with a loving heart and a pure motive. You will find that before a year is up you will be putting things from the list in the back of the book onto your thanksgiving list.

About a year after *Your Miracle Book* was published a man attending one of my lectures asked if he might say something. I invited him up to the platform and he said that he had purchased one of the first copies of *Your Miracle Book*. He said that his first three desires he had always before considered to be hopeless. However, he had decided to enter them in the book. Here are his desires:

1. That he (an insurance man) sell enough insurance to make the Million Dollar Round Table.
2. That he win a prize that his Insurance Company was then offering—a trip to Europe for two.
3. That his wife who was highly skeptical become interested in his church.

Again he reiterated that, at the time, it was hard for him to imagine any of these things happening. However, he said that he persisted, following the plan step by step and before the year was out he had made the Million

Dollar Round Table, he and his wife had just returned from the trip to Europe fully paid for by his company, and the following Sunday his wife was going to be received as a member of his church. His wife, seated beside him, beamed happily as he said this.

The minister of a large city church gave *Your Miracle Book* to the members of the congregation and invited them to write in their demonstrations. Somewhere in my files I have a file that is bulging with these exciting stories, each one more miraculous than the last.

Remember, miracles are *law-abiding events.* If you follow the law, believing, you will have a miracle—or, what will seem to be a miracle to you.

Nothing is too wonderful to happen, nothing is too good to be true. You can be healed. You can be delivered out of any difficulty known to man through spiritual mind treatment.

A CONTEMPLATIVE MEDITATION

> *Look unto me, and be ye saved, all the ends of the earth: for I am God, and there is none else.*—Isaiah 45:22

I turn from all the petty struggles in my world and the world around me. As I contemplate the Infinite, I am lifted into a new dimension of freedom. In consciousness, all that God is becomes mine to experience. That which my conscious awareness embodies becomes my experience.

Turning from fear and discouragement, I contemplate God as Love, a Love that will never leave me nor forsake me, a Love that is infinite and everywhere present. Love desires my highest good and perfects all that concerns me. Love comforts me, forgives me, and restores my soul. Love is the answer to my every need. As I contemplate Love, It flows forth into my experience and every moment is blessed.

Turning from any sense of lack or inadequacy, I contemplate God as Life. The earth is the Lord's and the fullness thereof. In the fullness of Life I live and naught is denied me. Nothing can limit Life as It lives through me. Life is never used up. Life never dies. Life is complete and perfect and this Life is my life to live.

Contemplating God, I contemplate my own true self made in the image and likeness of God. I am an expression of the Infinite and as I let It live through me, all problems are dissolved.

And so it is.

# THE TIME FOR MIRACLES IS NOW

*Jack Ensign Addington*

What is a miracle? A miracle is any dramatic change that appears to be supernatural because it is beyond explanation.

Are miracles occurring today? Can miracles occur in your life? This book shows that miracles are indeed happening today, and that a common denominator runs through them all. Anyone who understands that common denominator and how to use it may himself experience a miracle.

Dr. Addington says: "I live with miracles all the time. I have seen so many that they no longer surprise me, although I am continually thrilled to watch the miracle-working Power at work in the universe."

*The Time for Miracles Is Now* shows how the Power of the Universal Mind and the Spirit of Truth within you can lead you to make the right decisions and be instrumental in healing yourself and others.